THE WAY OF THE DISCIPLE

ERASMO LEIVA-MERIKAKIS

The Way of
the Disciple

IGNATIUS PRESS   SAN FRANCISCO

Cover art: *Christ and Saint Menas*
Tempera on wood, 7th–8th century, Coptic
Photo: Hervé Lewandowski
Louvre, Paris, France
© Réunion des Musées Nationaux/Art Resource, New York

Cover design by Roxanne Mei Lum

© 2003 Ignatius Press, San Francisco
All rights reserved
ISBN 978-0-89870-935-3 (PB)
ISBN 978-1-68149-568-2 (eBook)

Library of Congress Control Number 2002112862
Printed in the United States of America ∞

*A Nuestra Señora de la Caridad del Cobre
Patrona de Cuba, Madre de los discípulos,
y a su querida hija mejicana, Mireya,
que mora en mis entrañas*

CONTENTS

Καὶ ἐποίησεν δώδεκα ἵνα ὦσιν μετ᾽ αὐτοῦ.

And he created twelve that they might BE with him.

Mark 3:14

PREFACE

O NLY THE FULLNESS of the Gospel can succeed in portraying the way of the disciple in its totality, according to the mind of Christ. Anything else can only be an approximation, intended to examine more closely this or that particular aspect of Christian discipleship. Readers of this book will understandably ask themselves why I have chosen these particular passages of the Gospel, and not others, in order to elaborate on their basis a meditation on discipleship that may prove of help at least to some persons desirous to answer the call of Jesus. Where are the multiplications of loaves and fishes? Where are the Sermon on the Mount and the commission to Peter? Where is the Last Supper or the Agony in the Garden? Where is Calvary itself, or any event surrounding the Resurrection? Where, above all, is any scene specifically presenting the calling of disciples by Jesus?

Here I can only plead two things. First, that this little volume makes no claim whatsoever to presenting a complete theology of discipleship. And, second, that those who contemplate the Gospel text with the eyes of a faithful lover can, with patience, begin to discover the whole in the fragment, the full Mystery of Christ hidden in each and every scene. Then, too, I have deliberately avoided dealing with those scenes that have tended to be viewed as moments of special vocation to "professional" discipleship, because I believe that the call to discipleship in Christianity is universal and does not pertain to a select few. In other words, I would stress that every scene in the Gospel is about discipleship quite simply because the Gospel as such is *kerygma*—a proclamation of encounter with Christ inviting to faith in him and, consequently, to discipleship. If we have ears attuned to his voice and hearts willing to learn what his Heart has to teach, in every line of the Gospel we will hear Christ calling us to enter into his intimacy and destiny as disciples.

The brief epilogue from Blessed Ælred's "Sermon on the Annunciation" is meant to sum up in eloquent and prayerful form, as nourishment for the reader's way, the theme that runs all through these meditations: the fact that, if any one of us can hear the voice of Jesus calling, if any one of us can manage to drop the nets we happen to be mending at the moment in order to follow Jesus without reserve, this is only because he has first come to us and cast his saving glance upon us, has first taken upon himself the whole of our human condition and thus made himself our Emmanuel, the God who loves to dwell with his people as one of his people. Discipleship, then, is an integral part of the Mystery of the Incarnation, one of the choicest fruits borne by the deifying union of God and man in him who is Son of God and Mary.

Even a slender book like this does not come into being without the encouragement and aid of a considerable number of persons. Very special thanks go to those who asked me to break the bread of the Word with them on the subject of discipleship. It is beautiful to note that enthusiasm for the radical following of the Lord Jesus Christ may be amply witnessed not only in the monastic but also in the parish setting. I am very grateful to my dear friend Monsignor Felipe Estévez and the parish community of Saint Agatha's church (Miami, Florida) for their warm hospitality and joyful reception of my words. It is indeed a thrill to watch a laity in love with God, coming to the banquet of the Word in the evening after a long day of work, certainly fatigued and yet finding interior renewal in the communal contemplation of God's light shining on Jesus' face.

I would also like to thank, in the persons of their superiors, three communities of Cistercian nuns whose friendship in Christ is a gift I deeply treasure: Mother Gail Fitzpatrick, O.C.S.O. (Our Lady of the Mississippi Abbey, Dubuque, Iowa), Mother Agnes Day, O.C.S.O. (Mount Saint Mary's Abbey, Wrentham, Massachusetts), and Mother Miriam Pollard, O.C.S.O. (Santa Rita Abbey, Sonoita, Arizona). All of these communities provided me with an oasis for prayer and a readiness of heart and mind that made each of our encounters a truly palpable experience of Christ in our midst. Though I went to give talks, I walked away from each monastery enriched with far more than I brought there—things that paper cannot hold.

For reasons not directly connected with this book but that have made a crucial difference in my life, I would like to thank two communities of brothers I hold dear: Dom

Brendan Freeman, O.C.S.O., and the monks of New Melleray Abbey (Peosta, Iowa) extended to me a welcome that deeply stirred the heart, while Fathers Thomas McLaughlin, O.S.A., and Thomas Whelan, O.S.A., of the little Augustinian community on Cole Street in San Francisco, welcomed me with warm and simple generosity to their daily evangelical round of communal prayer, fellowship and breaking of bread. And the steady companionship of Father Blaise Berg, Father Owen Carroll, Sharane and Peter Darlington, Sister Monica Lawry, O.S.B., Jonathan Montaldo, and Father Stephen Verbest, O.C.S.O., has proven to be a source of much-needed strength.

In the end, however, my greatest thanks go to those who, by their sheer goodness and luminous presence in my life, have made me yearn to be a better disciple of the Lord Jesus. I speak, of course, of my children: Christiane, Adriana, Alexis, Chiara, Alicia, Isabel, Michael, and Jorge.

But my last and sweetest word must always be *Mireya*: Mireya at my beginning and, at my end, Mireya: for, in the perfect loveliness of Mireya's face and heart has shone for me the very Face of God.

Erasmo Leiva-Merikakis
Feast of Saint Bernard of Clairvaux
August 20, 2002

BECOMING WET CLAY
IN HIS HANDS

W HEN JESUS one day showed his apostles how to bring in an overwhelming catch of fish, Peter's reaction was to fall down at Jesus' knees and exclaim: "Depart from me, for I am a sinful man, O Lord."[1] But Peter's reaction was very different on the occasion when Jesus presented himself to the world as the Bread of Life and many found the teaching difficult and began to turn their backs on him. As the Lord pointedly asked the Twelve, " 'Will you also go away?' Simon Peter answered him, 'Lord, to whom shall we go? You have the words of eternal life.' "[2] These are indeed the two apparently opposite impulses that define the essence of discipleship: on the one hand, the consciousness of one's utter unworthiness to abide in the presence of the holy God and, simultaneously, one's desperate need precisely to abide in that presence, only source of lasting life and joy.

A Hassidic story has it that one time Rabbi Mordechai of Lechowitz was praying the psalm verse, "I was dumb

---

[1] Lk 5:8. Scriptural quotations are taken from the Revised Standard Version, unless otherwise noted.

[2] Jn 6:67–68.

and ignorant, I have been like a dumb beast in Your presence",[3] when he suddenly interrupted the psalm and exclaimed: "Lord of the world, dumb is what I want to be, I want to be a dumb beast, if only I may abide in Your presence."[4] The rabbi's moving plea would appear to reconcile the disciple's contradictory impulses of wanting at the same time to flee from and cling to the Lord. Obviously, the condition for abiding at the side of the Master of Life is that one be willing to shatter all illusions about the self's importance, wisdom, and general accomplishments and put on joyfully the truer identity of a "dumb beast". It was an ass, after all, that was privileged to bear the Lord Jesus on his back in his triumphal entry into Jerusalem!

We will see that the passion for simply abiding in the company of Jesus, the need continually *to be with him* in every sense of that verb, is the very heart of discipleship. But how does one become a disciple? What various stages of initiation does Christian discipleship include? Does the initiative in this process primarily reside with the disciple's desires or with the Teacher's election? What is the goal of long-term discipleship of Jesus? Before contemplating these and other specific aspects of discipleship, drawn from particular Gospel scenes, we must first address the prerequisite attitude for becoming in earnest a disciple of Christ: namely, the willingness to abandon

[3] Ps 72:22–23, translated from the original German.

[4] Martin Buber, *Die Erzählungen der Chassidim* (Zürich: Manesse Verlag, 1949), 625.

the old, what is behind us, and begin to desire to be created again by the power of God's Holy Spirit. An excellent orientation for this transformation comes from Saint Paul's Letter to the Ephesians, in a passage that summarizes many of the themes we will be examining at greater length:

> [May] the God of our Lord Jesus Christ, the Father of glory, . . . give you a spirit of wisdom and of revelation in the knowledge of him, having the eyes of your hearts enlightened, that you may know what is the hope to which he has called you, what are the riches of his glorious inheritance in the saints, and what is the *immeasurable greatness of his power* in us who believe, according to the *working of his great might* which he accomplished in Christ when he raised him from the dead and made him sit at his right hand in the heavenly places. . . . [The Father] has made [Christ] the head over all things for the church, which is his body, the fulness of him who fills all in all.[5]

Note here, first of all, how faith is the beginning of a work of transformation and enlightenment, the work of God's Spirit in us, accomplishing in us what has already been accomplished in Christ. In other words, his own glorious destiny is ours, too, a truth that climaxes liturgically in the feast of our Lady's Assumption and glorification: the Resurrection of the Son has already worked its full effect in the Mother who bore him in faith and love, and this, too, is our own path and destiny if we

[5] Eph 1:17–22; emphasis mine.

want it to be and if we are willing to live accordingly. Secondly, note also how Paul exhausts the vocabulary of words signifying power in order to communicate the intensity and depth of God constantly at work within us.

Whenever we come together to listen to the Word of God, what we are seeking at bottom is not mental information or moral instruction or even a sentimental influence that will make us "feel" the presence and goodness of God. What we seek with all our soul, rather, is the possibility of opening ourselves up in prayer to God's transforming action. Whether we are fully conscious of it or not, in other words, we desire a change of life, a conversion from what we presently are to a more precise embodiment of the likeness of Christ at the center of our being, radiating out from us through all our thoughts, words, and actions. This is why the life of contemplation is the boldest and most adventuresome of undertakings, for what could be more radical, more truly earth-shattering, than the willingness to be dismantled and created anew, not once or twice in a lifetime, but day after day? "If any one is in Christ, he is a new creation."[6] But being created in this sense is not a passive work. Our "clay" is the spiritual stuff of our will and freedom and thoughts and feelings and desires, and all of these have to be surrendered every day anew to God's power. We cannot become new creations without actively participating in our remaking by the Holy Spirit.

[6] 2 Cor 5:17.

Another name for God's transforming power in his Spirit is the Glory of God. Whenever God's Glory—the power and beauty and eternity of the God and Father of our Lord Jesus Christ—becomes manifested in our world and lives, it is not in order to destroy, supplant, and discard but in order to purify, transform, and vivify. God's Glory is the eternal power of God communicated to us creatures in order that we may come to share in the very life and bliss of God. God's Glory approaches us, not to obliterate us, but to house us: "For over all the glory there will be a canopy and a pavilion. It will be for a shade by day from the heat, and for a refuge and a shelter from the storm and rain."[7] But the only thing that God's Glory can house within itself is the persons God created us to be, and not the illusory selves we have manufactured; and so this Glory will often feel like a "consuming fire", separating the gold of our authentic, God-created being from the dross of our fake self-constructed image.

Nothing created can become housed within God's holiness without its first having to undergo serious transformation. Jesus says to us, "These things I have spoken to you, that my joy may be in you, and that your joy may be full",[8] and also, "Peace I leave with you; my peace I give to you"[9]—and we are naturally consoled. But do we truly have the strength and capacity for receiving and containing the joy and the peace that are the very life

[7] Is 4:5–6.
[8] Jn 15:11.
[9] Jn 14:27.

of God? The Letter to the Hebrews, even while contemplating the perfect sacrifice of Christ that we can now offer to the Father, nevertheless renews the Deuteronomic warning that "Our God is a consuming fire."[10] We are painfully aware that much in us is straw and that each of us will, along the way of discipleship, unavoidably "be salted with the fire" of the Holy Spirit.[11] How, then, shall our house of straw contain his fiery joy and peace?

Very enlightening in this regard is Psalm 68 ("*Let God arise, let his enemies be scattered . . .*"), a so-called "psalm of enthronement" sung by the Jews as the ark of the covenant—symbolic presence of God's Glory—was carried in solemn procession into the temple. Such psalms seem to some today to be merely historical records of ancient rites, expressing an archaic spirituality wholly irrelevant to us moderns, who have, after all, managed to invent "a more positive image of God". I think, however, that such psalms are fundamental to revelation, to our seeing how God really deals with us in our fallenness and need for re-creation:

> As wax melts before fire,
> let the wicked perish before God!
> But let the righteous be joyful;
>   let them exult before God;
>   let them be jubilant with joy!

[10] Heb 12:29 = Deut 4:24.
[11] Cf. Mk 9:49.

Sing to God, sing praises to his name;
lift up a song to him who rides upon the clouds;
his name is the LORD, exult before him!

Father of the fatherless and protector of widows
is God in his holy habitation.
God gives the desolate a home to dwell in;
he leads out the prisoners to prosperity;
but the rebellious dwell in a parched land.[12]

We should take note here of all the vital elements of a theophany (a manifestation on earth of the personal presence of the Lord God): Here are fire, power, the mysterious cloud, things bound to induce fear and awe; and yet these elements do not behave as we ordinarily know them in nature, because *here* they are at the same time a destructive threat to the wicked and a power of protection and renewed life to the humble and needy. God's holiness simultaneously shatters arrogance and makes the just rejoice. This is a great mystery. The psalm is a glorious expression of God's almighty presence, and it celebrates the fact that God's omnipotence always works through compassion. It is precisely God's Glory that makes him the Father of the destitute. His Glory becomes their shelter, their home, their destined abode for all eternity.

Our business, then, as Christians and as contemplatives —perhaps our *only* business—is to work tirelessly at becoming destitute and needy orphans and widows who rely only on the mercy, goodness, and power of God.

[12] Ps 68:2–6.

But is this not perhaps too nonsensical a statement in our age of great accomplishments, when all are dreaming of becoming masters of the world, or at least of as much of it as possible? "Christ . . . became poor," says Saint Paul, "so that by his poverty you might become rich."[13] But how can Christ enrich us if we are already rich by our own efforts, if we keep on building bigger and bigger silos to store away our own precious accomplishments with a kind of ecstatic greed?[14] And, even if we are materially poor and unambitious, do we still not tend to practice a kind of *spiritual* greed? A test would be to ask myself whether I can really be poor, silent, and joyous while at prayer in the presence of the Beloved, or whether I come to him only to win him over to my own thousand projects and desires. Can Christ really approve of this inner busyness of mine without in some sense ceasing to be Lord? What do we prefer, in the end, our own self-acquired wealth or the beautiful poverty of Christ? The Cistercian John of Ford, for one, exclaimed that he desired nothing other than to rest with Jesus at the center of his own poverty, the special place where Jesus had chosen to meet him.

If our vision and hearing and heart are polluted, prejudiced, shut off, we will surely not be able to behold the Glory of God. Indeed, "the Word became flesh and dwelt among us . . . ; we have beheld his glory", but at the same time: "He came to his own home, and his own

[13] 2 Cor 8:9.
[14] Cf. Lk 12:13–21.

people received him not."[15] What tells me into which of these two categories I fall? *Beholding* God's Glory is an act closely related to *receiving* the incarnate Word; and, in his First Letter, John prompts us to ask ourselves how we can love God, whom we do not see, if we do not love our brother, whom we do see.[16] Therefore, seeing God's Glory is intimately related as well to my ability to love the Word who has become incarnate in my brothers and sisters.

It is in order to become capable of all this that we must return time and again to the Creator's hands, return to the darkness of the cenacle in Jerusalem between the Ascension and Pentecost, return to the cave of Bethlehem —place of hidden adoration—return to the Lord's tomb and abide within its marvelous emptiness, return continually to the womb of the Church, there to be reshaped by the same Spirit that conceived Jesus in the womb of Blessed Mary. Christian life is at bottom about being continually rejuvenated and re-created by the power of the Spirit; but this cannot happen automatically: we must *want* to be made young and new again and coöperate in this process.

Such images, compelling as they are, have to receive very concrete translation and application in our particular needs and circumstances, both as individuals and as members of a community. We cannot be happy with just considering a beautiful, inspiring image at arm's length.

[15] Jn 1:14, 11.
[16] Cf. 1 Jn 4:20.

The authentic Christian is the person whose heart is perpetually open like the good earth to receive all these seeds of the Word into itself and to water them with tears of love and compunction and desire, in order to allow them to come to full harvest in the Lord's sight.

Consider in this connection two key passages from the first pages of Genesis:

> In the beginning God created the heavens and the earth. The earth was without form and void, and darkness was upon the face of the deep; and the Spirit of God was moving over the face of the waters.
>
> And God said, 'Let there be light'; and there was light. And God saw that the light was good.[17]

> But a mist went up from the earth and watered the whole face of the ground—then the LORD God formed man of dust from the ground, and breathed into his nostrils the breath of life; and man became a living being.[18]

In both places we see that, at the very beginning of God's creation, *water* is an essential element. Absence of water will always be the biblical symbol of the soul's need for redemption, the condition in which the clay of my being—once mixed with the water of the Spirit's grace —has become desiccated through sin and indifference: dry, rigid, brittle, dead as bones. If I put myself in God's hands in this state, his mighty touch would not shape me; it would destroy me and return me to mere dust, as

[17] Gen 1:1–4a.
[18] Gen 2:6–7.

Psalm 68 states: "Let God arise, let his enemies be scattered; let those who hate him flee before him!" We must pray with G. M. Hopkins, "Lord, send my roots rain", pray to become like wax before the advancing fire of his holiness, wax that is only too glad to be changed by heat into a new and more useful shape, glad even perhaps to be consumed as it feeds the beauty of a burning, light-giving flame.

Where in my own life and experience have I found that spring of water in the midst of the garden of Eden that makes it possible for God to shape the Adam in me into a living being by softening the clay of the ground and making it malleable, responsive to the divine Sculptor's hands? We must discover, at the center of the garden of our lives, the hidden spring of water that God has surely hidden there! We must continually return to it like the Samaritan woman to her well. Discovering that deep well within ourselves is perhaps the central activity of our spiritual search. That discovery goes hand in hand with my response to what the Lord says to us through Jeremiah: "Like the clay in the potter's hand, so are you in my hand, O house of Israel."[19] The hidden spring must water the clay of my being for as long as I am on that potter's wheel.

That "mist" welling up out of the earth and watering all the surface of the ground,[20] which makes the formation of man possible in the very next verse, must rep-

[19] Jer 18:6.
[20] Gen 2:6.

resent *the love of God* being poured out over all creation and animating all things so that they can have life and being in themselves. Without being watered continually by God's love, each thing hardens, becomes static, fossilized, as Psalm 68:9 again has it: "Rain in abundance, O God, you did shed abroad; you did restore your heritage as it languished." Even after Adam's creation, that water has to continue irrigating his being and our own; otherwise it becomes "dehydrated" and hardens again into dust. We see, then, the relevance of water as one of the chief symbols and sacramental means in Christianity: our baptism is an ongoing event.

A particularly poignant form that water takes, especially in the monastic tradition, is tears. Is this only a distant allusion to some golden era in monastic history, or are there ever real tears of repentance or of joy in my own prayer? For tears are the humble, created water of my heart that corresponds to the powerful uncreated water of the Spirit's life in me. Tears are perhaps the most rejuvenating and re-creating water of all, the evidence that I have allowed grace to melt the ice at the center of my being. As Léon Bloy says strikingly, where there are tears, there is the Holy Spirit, because the Spirit of God is always, as at the beginning, "hovering over the waters". What areas of my life are still rigid, refusing to yield resistance and be shaped by God's fingers? "Flecte quod est rigidum", we pray in the *Veni, sancte Spiritus*. In what parts of my person do I still allow the old inflexible grouch of sin to have his way? Each one of us, according to our state in life, has different strategies for allowing the old Adam and Eve to survive in us. We may have that rascal, the decrepit old self, locked away safely, but surreptitiously we still pass him food through the slot in the dungeon door, do we not?

The Glory of God is always found in movements of love, in communication of life, never in static routine, cramped piety, thoughtless repetition of official acts, conventional observance, external religious acts that could easily become the letter that kills, the continuing tyranny of the old, sinful self. The Spirit, by contrast, is wind, fire, light, water, Glory: the unexpected, the transforming, the self-communicating, the self-outpouring Power that shapes by embracing and not letting go. The way of the disciple is necessarily a way of discipline, because discipleship is the living school in which we *learn* how to be like Christ by intimate association with him. The discipline of Christian life, whether in its secular or its monastic form, is supposed to provide a structure that systematically excludes all the pseudo-adventures and pseudo-fulfillments offered by a frivolous world. Christian discipline is there to open the way for the real adventure of the soul's quest for God and God's quest for the soul, and it would be tragic if instead this discipline became its own end.

Can we, like our Lady, become a "temple of the Spirit's glory"[21] and a "house of divinity"?[22] Can Jesus be "glo-

[21] Collect, Tuesday, Seventh Week of Easter.
[22] Collect, December 20.

rified in us"[23] without our beginning to show qualities such as his own joyful freedom in service of the Father? How can I tell when the fire of the Holy Spirit continues to burn within me or when I have managed to half-extinguish it, perhaps, ironically, by a certain kind of religious routine? How can I expect to be embraced by God *as I am* if I will not embrace my sister and brother unless they conform to the image of them I have myself created? Christian discipline should create a *space of freedom* within me, within the community. Does it instead at times result in a clutter of observances piled up on one another or the frozenness of a self-satisfied soul, like that of the farmer whose silos are full to bursting but whose grain is allowed to rot unshared and unused?

I take this, then, to be the foundation of serious Christian existence: the deliberate choice, repeated on a daily and hourly basis, to return to the beginning, to our own individual "genesis", to a state where God's Spirit may create us anew. Formlessness, darkness, indetermination, wet shapeless clay: Are these not the conditions for receiving the mercy of God in any way his wisdom may choose to give it to us? Was this not the situation of the apostles between the Ascension and Pentecost, a situation that serves as model for the permanent condition of the Church in the world?

In both the family and the monastery we have all had the individual and communal experience of a shattering

[23] Cf. Jn 17:10.

of the structures in our lives, structures that at one time we thought essential for our stability and even sanity. But when this happens we must believe in faith that God's providence is only creating something even better, something that would never have occurred to us in our limited and eccentric vision of things. I have always been fascinated by the Lord's statement to Peter: "When you were young, you girded yourself and walked where you would; but when you are old, you will stretch out your hands, and another will gird you and carry you where you do not wish to go."[24] Whimsical, wide-roaming freedom is characteristic of immaturity, of a youthful lack of purpose and direction.

Mature Christian freedom, by contrast, is my total availability and obedience to the will of the all-wise God. We may initially find any disciplinary structure difficult, but with time we may so internalize it and identify with it that it becomes a new and comfortably improved self-image. But that would be too bad, because this accommodation would defeat the purpose of Christian discipline as a permanent instrument of openness to the work of the Spirit within us. It is not enough by far to have taken radical initial steps of conversion and to be a reasonably observant and faithful Christian. At the center of our being we must remain poor and free and available to God, rather than barricade ourselves through habit to the approaches of God's ever-surprising grace.

[24] Jn 21:18.

These passages from Genesis, then, about darkness and water and clay in God's hands, evoke the Christian vigil in the night of the world; Christian renunciation of worldly projects and purpose; Christian tears of repentance that water the clay of our being, returning it to a state of malleability. Again, what is all of this but the decision to put ourselves back into the hands of the supreme Artist, that he may create us anew, giving us any shape that will best show Christ's face to the world here and now? Our only joy and peace lie in making ourselves available in this way to the power of his molding hands. As we pray at Vespers every day, "He looks on his servant in her lowliness." The Latin for "lowliness" here is *humilitas*, which evokes *humus* and the fruitfulness of wet, dark soil.

May we become like Mary our Mother, who made herself so deeply and consistently available to God's transforming love that in the end she was taken up body and soul into the very glory of the uncreated Trinity. In her, our own humanity is already made radiant, and so she is the permanent source of all our hope. For us, glorification through sharing God's immortality is not a mere ideal, a utopian dream, but a palpable reality. The destiny of the Mother is both unique to herself and yet also trail-blazing for us, her children, for no mother worthy of the name wants to enjoy a privilege from which her children will be excluded. But am I striving to find my joy where she found it?

By the very nature of what we are discussing here, it should be obvious that none of it can wait, that we can never take a vacation from it, for what is involved is not something optional, extracurricular, so to speak, but the very substance of our being and life. "O that to-day you would hearken to his voice! Harden not your hearts."[25] Today is all we have, today alone is real. Today is the beginning, when God creates again. His mercy and power and love are everlasting; they endure even after our own hearts and imaginations and willpower have long since given up. But this we can always do: make ourselves available to his hands, ever ready to mold.

Consider in this connection the following splendid text of Irenæus of Lyons. The context is his attempt to expose the error of the Gnostics, who taught that human beings are already divine just by virtue of their becoming aware of their spiritual nature:

> How could you be God, if you have not even yet been made into a man? How could you be perfect if you have only just been made? How could you be immortal if, having a mortal nature, you have not obeyed your Creator? For first you must retain your rank as man and only afterward receive a share in the glory of God: because it is not you who make God, but God who makes you. If, then, you are the work of God, wait patiently for the Hand of your Artist, who does all things at the opportune time. . . . Present him with a malleable and docile heart, and retain

[25] Ps 95:7–8.

the form the Artist has given you, keeping in yourself the water that comes from him and, lacking which, you would grow hard and reject the imprint of his fingers.

By keeping this shape, you will climb to perfection, because the art of God will cover over the clay that is in you. His Hand created your substance; it will clothe you with pure gold inside and out; it will adorn you so well that the King himself will fall in love with your beauty. But if, becoming hard, you reject his art and show yourself unhappy with his having made you a man, by your ingratitude toward God you will reject all at once both his art and life itself, for making is proper to God's goodness, and being made is proper to man's nature.

If, therefore, you give him what can come only from you, which is faith in him and submission to him, you will receive the benefit of his art, and you will be the perfect work of God. If, on the contrary, you resist him and flee his Hands, the cause of your unfinishedness will reside in you who have not obeyed, not in him who called you. For he sent out servants to invite [you] to the wedding banquet, but those who did not listen to him deprived themselves of the feast of the Kingdom.[26]

"Present him with a malleable and docile heart, and retain the form the Artist has given you, keeping in yourself the water that comes from him": the only way of doing this is to become ever more attentive, ever more docile. Pondering God's Word is the concrete manner

[26] Irenæus of Lyons, *Against the So-Called Gnosis* [*Against Heresies*], 4, 39, 2–3.

in which the soul becomes more and more malleable to the stress of God's hands. One cannot become a disciple without being attentive, without the ability and willingness to listen profoundly and perseveringly, really listen from the center of one's being to what is being said to him personally by God. This is easier said than done and is in fact quite impossible without the daily concrete attempt to practice attentive interior listening. In this connection, Simone Weil offers us superb practical advice:

Attention consists in suspending one's thought, in making oneself available, empty, and penetrable to the object contemplated. The wealth of knowledge one has already acquired and is forced to use must, at the moment of contemplative attention, be kept nearby, close to one's present thinking, but at an inferior level. With regard to all particular thoughts one has already formed, attentive thinking must be like a man on top of a mountain looking out before him. He is aware of the forests and plains before him and below him, but he does not really look at them. Above all, attentive thought must be empty, in expectation, not searching for anything, but ready to receive in all its naked truth the object that is to penetrate it. All misunderstandings . . . , all absurdities [in our efforts to express our view of the world] come from the fact that our thought has with too much haste jumped on something and has filled itself prematurely and thus is no longer available to receive the truth. The cause is always that one has wanted to be active; one has wanted to search. . . . But the most precious goods must not be searched for;

they must be waited for. Because man cannot find them by his own efforts, and if he goes out searching for them he will instead find false goods whose falsity he will not be able to discern.[27]

Attentiveness such as this is the concrete means that allows the water of grace to invade the clay of our hardened hearts and return them to that amorphous and therefore promising state of the first day of creation. It is then that God's Spirit and Life may be breathed into us again and that the dry bones of our being may again be clothed with vital muscle and skin. Let us hand ourselves over to the loving power of an ever-creating God, the God who will not accept half-measures and accommodations, because he is unfathomable holiness and wants nothing more than to plunge us into the depths of his own holy life.

---

[27] "Réflexions sur le bon usage des études scolaires en vue de l'Amour de Dieu" (Reflections on the Right Use of Scholastic Studies with a View to the Love of God), in: *Attente de Dieu* (Paris: Éditions Fayard, 1966), 92–93.

2

THE INVITATION:
"COME TO ME"

O UR THEME is discipleship, the intimate following of Jesus, and we will develop this subject on the basis of select Gospel episodes, each one of which will take us a little deeper into the knowledge of our Lord Jesus Christ and his Father. Before I go on to comment on specific Gospel passages, however, I must remind you of the warning given by Apa Theodore in Cassian's *Institutes*, a warning that should be sobering for both the teacher and his audience:

> The monk who wants to attain knowledge of the Scriptures should not waste his efforts on the books of the commentators, but should rather direct all the activity of his spirit and all the attention of his heart to the purification of the vices of the flesh. Once these have been driven out, and the veils of the passions have been lifted, the eyes of the heart will naturally contemplate the mysteries of the Scriptures. For the grace of the Holy Spirit has not taught these mysteries for them to remain unknown and dark; rather, they became such through our own fault, when we allow the veil of sin to darken the eyes of our heart. Once these have been restored to their natural health, the simple reading of Sacred Scripture amply suffices all by itself for the contemplation of true knowledge.[1]

[1] Cassian, *Instituta*, 5, 34.

The whole labor of the interpretation of Scripture, therefore, is intimately related to the ascetical life, to the effort, that is, to overcome the blindness that sin inflicts upon our soul. The quest to understand the mysteries of revelation is meaningless without an accompanying desire to change one's life so that our organs of interior perception may be restored to their pristine health.

A densely charged passage in Mark gives us the whole structure of authentic discipleship in a nutshell: "Jesus went up into the hills and called to him those whom he desired; and they came to him. And he created twelve, in order that they might be with him and to be sent out to preach and have authority to cast out demons."[2] Here we see at once the five elements that make up the reality of discipleship: (1) our solitude with Jesus, (2) his freedom in choosing and calling, (3) our response to the call, (4) the shared life of companionship with Jesus and the other disciples, and (5) the mission to teach and heal. It is noteworthy that, of these five elements, only the fifth involves any visible activity in the world; the other four are interior work and represent the substantial center of the disciple's experience, with the visible apostolate as fruit.

There is little doubt, then, that the disciple will spend the greater part of his time and effort, not "doing God's work", but simply in yielding to the work God wants to do in him. No one can be a disciple without first

[2] Mk 3:14-15, my translation.

being a contemplative. The heart of Jesus' intention in choosing his followers is *that they might be with him:* above all, Jesus wants to share his life with us, and this too— *the longing to be with Jesus*—should be the gravitational pull to which all our desires should hasten. The Greek phrase καὶ ἐποίησεν δώδεκα ἵνα ὦσιν μετ' αὐτοῦ used here is normally translated quite weakly. It does not say that Jesus merely "appointed" twelve apostles, but that he actually *made* (ἐποίησεν) those men into such. He transformed very ordinary and unpromising persons into active vessels of divine grace, a feat that only God himself can accomplish through a work that merits the name of *re-creation*. And the final goal of this transformation is first and foremost that the apostles "might be with him" (ἵνα ὦσιν μετ' αὐτοῦ), a strong purpose clause revealing the deepest mind and Heart of Jesus in the work of redemption. Now, this primordial purpose of the apostle's vocation to "be with Jesus" must by no means be construed in the sentimental sense of warm companionship and safe conduit to salvation. Rather, we must give the verb "to be" here its full ontological weight by understanding the divinely appointed goal to be nothing less than *deification*: If the apostles are called to be with Jesus, it is because they are called to become what Jesus already is—the perfect theandric unity of the divine and human natures. Ultimately, we are called to live the very life of God in and through our union of shared existence with the only-begotten Son.

Whatever Jesus may then want to draw out of our companionship with him for the life of the world, that will be his own work and decision as well. We have only to listen to the call, to respond by going to where Jesus is, and to take up our habitual abode by his side. No one can be sent by Jesus to heal the world who has not first been called out of the world by Jesus to his side in solitude. The going up into the hills represents the movement from this world to the Father, who alone is Jesus' own "native land". "Father, I desire that they also, whom you have given me, *may be with me* where I am, to behold my glory which you have given me in your love for me before the foundation of the world."[3]

If the disciples will eventually be able to bear credible witness to Jesus, this is only because of their intimate association with him apart from the world, in the shared solitude of daily companionship. In this the disciples share, amazingly, in the rôle of the Holy Spirit himself, and for the same reason: "The Spirit of truth, who proceeds from the Father, he will bear witness to me; and you also are witnesses, because *you have been with me* from the beginning."[4]

We must, then, come humbly to God's inspired written Word in the Gospel to allow him to reveal to us through it the presence and reality of his living Word. The written Word is but an echo of the living Word, God's Son Jesus Christ, whom he does not cease to speak into the world and our hearts. The table of the writ-

[3] Jn 17:24, emphasis mine.
[4] Jn 15:27, emphasis mine.

ten and proclaimed Word is never far from the table of Christ's Body and Blood. The full Christ is not simply the person we come to know vicariously through the text of the Gospel, but that person as we encounter him fully alive in the Word and Sacrament and Body of the Church. The human language concerning him is the call to come to the person of Jesus himself. The written Word, even when profoundly meditated upon, can at best bring us to the threshold of the living person of Jesus. Nothing can substitute for this personal encounter, this merging of the horizons of the person of Jesus with my own, this convergence of my and our existence with his, here and now.

To hear and conceive the Word of God presupposes our willingness to be dramatically changed in the center of who we are: Isaiah says that God's Word is like the rain, which does not return to heaven until it has done the work on earth that God has appointed to it,[5] and Hebrews warns us that "the word of God is living and active, sharper than any two-edged sword, piercing to the division of soul and spirit, of joints and marrow, and discerning the thoughts and intentions of the heart. And before him no creature is hidden, but all are open and laid bare to the eyes of him with whom we have to do."[6] In John's Gospel, Jesus affirms: "Every one who does evil hates the light, and does not come to the light, lest his deeds should be exposed. But he who does what

[5] Cf. Is 55:10–11.
[6] Heb 4:12–13.

is true comes to the light, that it may be clearly seen that his deeds have been wrought in God."[7] Now Christ is "the true light [who] . . . was coming into the world".[8]

Therefore, if we expose ourselves deeply and humbly to the power of God's Word, he will come to us as both rain and sword, as both principle of new life and fruition *and* as scalpel in the hand of a surgeon who must painfully cut if he is to heal. Only after it has inflicted pain can God's Word console. In Scripture, what we could call the "good news of damnation" is always the necessary prelude to the good news of salvation, as T. S. Eliot has stated in his essay on Baudelaire: "In an age of progressive degradation, Baudelaire perceived that what really matters is Sin and Redemption. . . . The recognition of the reality of Sin is a New Life, . . . damnation itself is an immediate form of salvation."[9] In the light of the Word our life comes under scrutiny, an examination that judges and induces change and transformation, something our nature instinctively abhors. Blessed be God, who has given us a desire for his love and truth that is far stronger than all the combined forces of our fallen nature, which recoils in horror at the prospect of thorough transformation.

[7] Jn 3:20–21.

[8] Jn 1:9.

[9] T. S. Eliot, *Selected Essays*, new ed. (New York: Harcourt, Brace, 1964), 378–79. The following verses of Baudelaire are a good illustration of what Eliot means: "Et mon cœur s'effraya d'envier maint pauvre homme / Courant avec ferveur à l'abîme béant, / Et qui, soûl de son sang, préférerait en somme / La douleur à la mort et l'enfer au néant" ("Le Jeu", in: *Les Fleurs du mal*, 96).

But who is this God, and how does he call us to discipleship, a "school" in which far more than just our minds are trained, a school in which we become new persons? We will begin fashioning an answer to this question by considering a passage in Matthew long familiar to all of us, but truly so central that it cannot be meditated upon too often:

> At that time Jesus declared: "I thank you, Father, Lord of heaven and earth, that you have hidden these things from the wise and understanding and revealed them to infants; yes, Father, for such was your gracious will. All things have been delivered to me by my Father; and no one knows the Son except the Father, and no one knows the Father except the Son and any one to whom the Son chooses to reveal him. Come to me, all who labor and are heavy laden, and I will give you rest. Take my yoke upon you, and learn from me; for I am gentle and lowly in heart, and you will find rest for your souls. For my yoke is easy, and my burden is light." [10]

This passage has been called the "pearl" of the Gospel of Matthew. It jumps up out of the surrounding text with great power of appeal. It disrupts the usual sequence of Matthew's narrative of Jesus' life and deeds as a great aside; and yet this "aside" is like the lifting up of a veil that for a moment allows us to behold the Face of God. The text literally begins, "At that time, Jesus *answered*", rather than "declared": as if this prayer and dialogue were

[10] Mt 11:25–30.

always ongoing in his life, regardless of what else is occurring at a more surface level. We see here that the relationship between Father and Son is what underlies every scene of the Gospel, and the solemn formula "at that
time" stresses the way in which, in Jesus, eternity has
burst into time. Regardless of what Jesus may be saying
and doing externally, we here see where his Heart is always simultaneously occupied: with thanksgiving and joy
in his Father, expressed in unceasing communion. When
inviting us to come to him, it is more precisely to his
joy in his Father that he is inviting us.

The passage begins with a prayer of Jesus to the Father that we are allowed to overhear; only then is an invitation extended to us. The marvelous thing about this
man, Jesus of Nazareth, is that, when we go to him, we
encounter not just a great (or even the greatest) human
being, but always God his Father, "the Lord of heaven
and earth". Jesus is a window to the freedom and vast-
ness of eternity, the entryway into the abyss of God's
trinitarian Being.

And yet a paradox is involved here: this greatness and
depth of God can be perceived only by babes, the *nêpioi* or
"infants"—those who have no words of their own—and
not by those who are wise and possess understanding according to the logic of the world. Not in vain does Saint
Bernard say, "Non consolatur Christi infantia garrulos"
—"Christ's infancy does not console the garrulous."[11]

---

[11] Bernard of Clairvaux, *Sermo 5 in Nativitate Domini*, 5.

To these—to mere babes, to those of innocent heart—
God reveals his inmost secrets as to his intimate friends
and dear children. There is a clear affinity between God
and children. This truth is at the center of the mystery of
Christmas, when God is revealed in the form of a baby.
More than mere "affinity", this is actual identification:
The eternal God becomes what he most loves on earth
—a child. But this is no mere sweet sentimentality on
God's part: If he loves the childlike, it is because they
are empty enough to receive what he wants to give, a
mystery that Guerric of Igny expounds with lyric power
in these two passages:

> The silence of the Word in the womb of the Virgin speaks
> to you, cries out to you, recommends the discipline of si-
> lence. For "in silence and in hope shall be your strength",
> as Isaiah promises,[12] who defined the pursuit of justice
> as silence. As the Christ-Child in the womb advanced to-
> ward birth in a long, deep silence, so does the discipline of
> silence nourish and form and strengthen a person's spirit,
> and produce growth which is safer and more wholesome
> for being the more hidden.[13]

> If in the depths of your soul you were to keep a quiet si-
> lence, the all-powerful Word would flow from the Father's
> throne secretly into you. Happy then is the person who
> has so fled the world's tumult, who has so withdrawn into

[12] Is 30:15.

[13] Guerric of Igny, *Sermon 28*, 5, in *Liturgical Sermons*, trans. Monks of
Mount Saint Bernard Abbey, Cistercian Fathers Series, vol. 31 (Kalamazoo: Cistercian Publications, 1971), 52.

the solitude and secrecy of interior peace, that he can hear not only the Voice of the Word, but the Word himself: not John but Jesus.[14]

The first effect of the advent of God's Word is thus to take away our own thoughts and words and fill us with the vision of God's own Heart. If Jesus himself speaks so familiarly with his Father, it is because he never ceases to be Son—loving, obedient, faithful Son—and his Father has eyes and heart only for those who resemble Jesus.

This Son is Lord only because he receives everything from his Father. The Son has nothing of his own, and therefore his Father can and must continually give him everything. Such is the rich poverty of Jesus, not only in his humble Incarnation, but already as the eternal Word in the Trinity, who does not speak for himself but *is always spoken* by Another. Thus, although the Son is himself God, he is the Person in the Godhead who receives, who is wholly open to receiving all, while the Father is the Person in the Godhead who generates and gives. Not only generating and giving is a divine quality, but also being generated and receiving.

Our Lady is the creature who most excellently mirrors this trinitarian mystery in her own being: "Blessed is she who believed that there would be a fulfillment of what was spoken to her from the Lord."[15] The great irony is

[14] Guerric of Igny, *Sermons*, 4, 2, in *Liturgical Sermons*, trans. by Monks of Mount Saint Bernard Abbey, Cistercian Fathers Series, vol. 8 (Kalamazoo: Cistercian Publications, 1970), 24.

[15] Lk 1:45.

that we, who are merely human, are usually too full of our own ideas, projects, desires, anxieties, and prejudices to be free enough to receive anything. Why is it that we instinctually think that the least idea that pops into our head is the most important thing in the world, something that must be urgently expressed or we will explode? Yes, while man is proud, God himself is humble! We do not appreciate to what extent Jesus has power, is wise, does good, and so on, solely because of his great simplicity of soul and perfect receptivity as Son. He never forgets who his Father is and that he himself is always Son, and therefore his Father can continually fill him with life and glory. In the same way that the eternal Son never desires ever to be anything but Son, so, too, his disciple never desires to be anything except, more and more, a disciple. Being a disciple of Jesus is the created mode of being a child of the eternal Father.

By inviting us to come to himself, Jesus is introducing us into his relationship with his Father. This relationship is the true gift he gives us. "No one knows the Son except the Father, and no one knows the Father except the Son and any one to whom the Son chooses to reveal him." If this is true, then Jesus' choice in freedom to reveal the Father precisely to us involves an event far more stupendous than we may at first realize, accustomed as we are to hearing this language. This revelation to us of the Father by Jesus brings us directly into the mainstream of the very life of God, who is not only "Lord of heaven and earth" but also the only Being whose existence is absolutely necessary. In Christ we are invited to become the intimates of the One without whom nothing else could have existence. We are to become friends of the Source of all that is.

The fundamental requirement for us to be admitted to such divine knowledge is that we become like little infants interiorly, that is, that we, at the deepest level, give up trying to generate our own meaning and to be lords and masters of our own lives, and instead begin living by faith in what God can do for us. The fundamental truth of God's reality as absolute Source has to be lived by each of us moment by moment, as our own deepest truth. Our sanctification consists in being willing to embrace with our actual lives the truth that already is found at the root of our existence: our creatureliness and utter dependence. Christian life means to continue always being created by God. No one can be a Christian without learning how to become totally dependent on God as Father, in union with Jesus as our brother and Mary as our mother.

All of Jesus' greatness comes paradoxically from his being Son and aspiring to be nothing but Son. Only as disciples of this Son can we hope to be adopted by the Father as children. This may be the toughest thing about being a Christian in an age where only power, individualism, success, and total independence are officially admirable. It is God's "gracious will" or "good pleasure" (*eudokia*) that we should put on the attitude of his devoted children. This good pleasure is the living bond between Son and Father and is, therefore, the Holy Spirit, the power that transforms us too into God's children.

And yet our nature rebels and wants to be autonomous (that is, to live by a law of its own devising) and autocratic (that is, to be a power unto itself). While God's good pleasure leads to our insertion into the community of Divine Persons, worldly autonomy leads to splendid isolation and eventually to death of soul, since it cuts off from the Source of life.

Spiritual childhood must not, however, be misinterpreted as perpetual infantilism or immaturity in the psychological sense, or as some kind of mental deficiency stupidly embraced. The kind of childlike dependence on the Father meant here can be understood only if we look at Jesus himself as a living example of what is meant. In him radical dependence on the Father and obedience to him enabled him to accomplish marvelously bold and vibrant things that are the opposite of limp indifference: to preach the truth, oppose tyrants, love and heal the poor and sick, teach the ignorant, die on the Cross to redeem the world, rise from the dead by his Father's power, send the Holy Spirit to re-create our hearts. Christian dependence on God produces attitudes and deeds of freedom, while most often the so-called "successful" people of this world labor under a slavery that puts glum looks on their faces and makes them prisoners of apathy. Children, on the other hand, so dependent on their parents, enjoy a freedom at play and a capacity for joy that adults normally lose, because adult "autonomy" mostly means establishing ourselves as God—an unnatural burden that is sure to crush us after a few initial thrills.

Those who "labor and are heavy laden" are all of

us. We have mysteriously accepted from any number of sources, or perhaps have also had foisted on us, images of success, strange identities, psychological burdens, and lifetime goals that are killing us with exhaustion and frustration. Can we think of what might be the specific versions of these unnatural burdens in our own lives, burdens from which Christ wants to liberate us? Adulthood, instead of freeing us, has often turned us into slaves —perhaps respectable, outwardly successful, highly educated—but nonetheless *slaves*. It seems that, if we do not recognize this about ourselves, then Jesus has not come for us, since he does not invite those who are rested and satisfied but those who need to have their crushing burdens lifted from their shoulders. None of us escapes the universal diagnosis of the divine Physician, and no one can accept the invitation who refuses first to accept the diagnosis. And here please note that we are not speaking of moral culpability and specific misdeeds but of something more hidden and chronic: we are speaking of the wounds of our nature, however they may have been inflicted, by ourselves or by others, and of our need to present them to God for healing.

The beginning of this relief is already contained in the fact that Jesus allows us to overhear his own intimate prayer of joyful thanksgiving to his Father before he turns to us with his invitation. The basis of our liberation must be found in our learning how to turn to the Father with Jesus, as he does here, with great joy coming from humility and the recognition that, before God, we must be nothing other than babbling children. *This* is what Jesus' disciple must learn, the freedom of the babbling child on his Father's lap. Jesus' "Come to me" is, in fact, a fulfillment of Isaiah's prophecy: "You shall suck [of my prosperity], you shall be carried upon [my] hip, and dandled upon [my] knees. As one whom his mother comforts, so I will comfort you."[16]

True, Jesus "gives us rest". But we must be clear that such "rest" is totally different from "resting up" in order to get back to the daily toils of life, different, too, from recreation or distraction or vacationing, all of which are ordered to getting back to the "serious" part of life. It seems to me that this "rest for our souls" is intended by Jesus to be a real and genuine *state of life*, the natural condition in which a child of God habitually exists, and not just a passing phase of recovery. It is a deep condition of soul that is quite compatible with all the ordinary exterior activities and efforts of human life. The one who truly becomes God's child, like Jesus, enjoys such rest as the very element of existence in which he swims.

This rest is not laziness or a restoration of energy in order to get back to serious work: it is an end in itself, a way of life rooted in the relationship to God as Father. Such rest is utter trust actually lived out moment by moment. But because it calls for the asceticism of continual surrender, it has been called *laboriosa quies*, "rest that requires effort". To rest in this way means to allow the

[16] Is 66:12–13.

Father continually to be giving us his life, to have nothing
come from our own devising, to allow God full room for
acting as the true Creator of our being. These are things
that the slave cannot understand, since for him carrying
absurd burdens is what is normal. Only the child sees it
as normal for his father to care continuously for his freedom and needs and welfare.

But this rest that Jesus gives to those who become like
him itself has a condition: "Take *my* yoke upon you and
learn from me." He does take away the burden of our
slavery to artificial ideals, social conventions, materialis-
tic values, the cult of pleasure and of the body, and any
number of obsessions; but he does this only in order to
give a yoke of his own. It is clear that as creatures we
are always going to be serving some "master" or other:
it can be society, individual persons, a certain powerful
group, some idea we are obsessed with, or perhaps our
own tyrannical and capricious will in the form of addic-
tion to money, possessions, sex, drugs, alcohol, or simply
to the thrill of power and success. Clearly, any of these
can be a cruel tyrant, and we will be poor slaves laboring
under its tyranny. *Or* we can serve and share the labor
of him who is "gentle and lowly of heart", the Son who
invites us to intimacy with the Father by our sharing his
own destiny and mission.

Saint Bernard has left us an unparalleled exploration of
this crucial issue of our choice of "burdens". The passage
more than merits prolonged meditation:

Man seeks to imitate his Creator in a perverse way, so that as God is for himself his own law and depends on himself alone, so does man want to govern himself and make his own will his law. This heavy and unbearable yoke weighs on all Adam's sons, alas making us curve our necks and bend down so that our life seems to draw near hell (cf. Ps 87:4). . . . The soul struggling under this load laments, saying: "Why have you, [O God,] set me against you, and I am become a burden for myself?"[17] By the words "I am become a burden for myself" is shown that he himself is his own law and that nobody but himself did that. But what he said previously, speaking to God: "Why have you set me against you", means that he has not escaped from God's law. It is proper to God's eternally just law that he who does not want to accept its sweet rule, will be the slave of his own will as a punishment; he who casts away the pleasant yoke and light load of charity,[18] will have to bear unwillingly the unbearable burden of his own will. . . . He can neither escape the law of justice which he deserves nor remain with God in his light, rest and glory, because he is subject to power and banished from happiness. O Lord, my God, "why do you not take away my sin, and wherefore do you not remove my evil,"[19] that delivered from the heavy load of self-will, I may breathe under charity's light burden . . . ? Those who follow what the Apostle says, "May you owe nobody anything unless it be to love one another,"[20] without a doubt they are in

[17] Job 7:20.
[18] Cf. Mt 11:30.
[19] Job 7:21.
[20] Rom 13:8.

this world as God is, neither slaves nor hirelings but [free] sons [of God their Father].[21]

"Take my yoke upon you": Note the freedom of choice involved here. In other cases the yoke of slavery is something cruelly and insidiously imposed on us against our better will and understanding. The proposal here by Jesus is open and frank: "First see who I am," he seems to be saying, "consider my heart of hearts, understand my origin in the Father and my mission among you to reveal his love and goodness, and only then decide for yourselves whether or not you want to become my intimate companions, friends, and collaborators." Here, at the very least, we have a choice of lords, and this one Lord, Jesus, is offering to share with us the yoke of his own sonship, which is that of his gentle and lowly Heart and which, as such, can impose only burdens deriving from the sweetness of truth and love. As Bernard again exclaims: "Sic onerat me miserationibus suis Deus, sic concludit, sic obruit me beneficiis suis, ut onus aliud sentire non possim" ("God has so laden me with his tender mercies, so encompassed, so overwhelmed me with his benefits, that I am unable to feel any other burden.")[22]

Serve we surely will; but the crucial question is: Whom or what will we serve? The tyrant who day by day sucks

[21] Bernard of Clairvaux, *On Loving God*, 36, trans. Robert Walton, Cistercian Fathers Series, vol. 13 (Kalamazoo: Cistercian Publications, 1995), 128–29.

[22] Bernard of Clairvaux, *Sermones varii*, "De misericordiis", opening, trans. by a priest of Mount Melleray.

out the substance of my soul, mind, and body, or the Lord whose yoke is easy and whose burden is light? If we have any doubts about the difference between serving the Lord God and the monarchs of this world, we have only to turn to the passage in which the prophet Samuel is warning Israel of what will come from her insistence on having an earthly king ruling over her:

> These will be the ways of the king who will reign over you: he will take your sons and appoint them to his chariots and to be his horsemen, and to run before his chariots; and he will appoint for himself commanders of thousands and commanders of fifties, and some to plow his ground and to reap his harvest, and to make his implements of war and the equipment of his chariots. He will take your daughters to be perfumers and cooks and bakers. He will take the best of your fields and vineyards and olive orchards and give them to his servants. He will take the tenth of your grain and of your vineyards and give it to his officers and to his servants. He will take your menservants and maidservants, and the best of your cattle and your asses, and put them to his work. He will take the tenth of your flocks, and you shall be his slaves. And in that day you will cry out because of your king, whom you have chosen for yourselves; but the LORD will not answer you in that day.[23]

"You shall be his slaves": Indeed, while tyrannical lords want to oppress us, to exploit us, and then to discard us, the Lord Jesus wants to associate us with himself so that,

[23] 1 Sam 8:11–18.

little by little, we may come to resemble him more and more by learning from his person. Here we see the reason why Christ provides the foundation for the only authentic humanism worthy of the name, and why monastic life should represent in the Church the very form of Christian humanism, since it has made of interior freedom for love's sake an institutional way of life. Here lies the only true way of coming to know God, which we have said is equivalent to possessing eternal life.

We come to know God by associating intimately, step by step, with Jesus his Son, and as we grow in intimacy with Jesus he can reveal to us his intimate life with his Father. To know who God is can come only from personal, long-time association and cohabitation with Jesus. And, if his "yoke is easy, [his] burden light", it is because it is shared with him, because he never asks anything of us that he, the eternal Word, is not himself already doing. We are invited to a literally *con-jugal* relationship with Jesus, one in which we share with him his own yoke (*jugum*) of obedience, through which he redeems the world.

What kind of Lord is this, who wants nothing more than to give us everything that he has and is, a Lord in whom power and goodness utterly coincide? The world has never seen his like before. Indeed, since he is the only Son of God and by rights possesses all the treasures of wisdom, joy, and power his Father possesses, Jesus apparently wants nothing more than to share these treasures with us by granting us a share in his very sonship. Who would not fall in love with such a Lord out of sheer gratitude? Who would not gladly embrace the Cross, which is the truer name for his God-imposed "yoke"? In drastic contrast to the tyrants of this world, who exert power over others solely for their own selfish benefit, it is "for freedom [that] Christ has set us free", and not for his own gain. "Stand fast therefore, and do not submit again to a yoke of slavery",[24] whether this yoke is imposed by others or by our own tyrannical self.

May Jesus transform us gradually into the utterly free and utterly obedient person he already is and has been from all eternity.

[24] Gal 5:1.

3

FOLLOWING THE
HOMELESS ONE

W E MUST NOW go from the general to the particular, from hearing Jesus' generous invitation, "Come to me", to the specific path that our feet must tread if we are to live out that invitation. We will pursue the theme of following Jesus wherever he goes in the light of the episode of the storm on the lake in Matthew 8:18–27.

Rarely do we take note of how eminently a paschal theme the concrete following of Jesus is. And yet his call to us cannot be understood outside the context of God's command to the Jews through Moses that they should sacrifice a paschal lamb, leave Egypt, cross the Red Sea, and seek the Promised Land after a very long sojourn during which they would have to endure all the hardships of the desert. "The Lamb in the midst of the throne will be their shepherd, and he will guide them to springs of living water", we read in the Apocalypse,[1] which also tells us that the 144,000 who will be saved are the ones who "follow the Lamb wherever he goes".[2] On the twelve foundations of the City of God are to be read

[1] Rev 7:17.
[2] Rev 14:4.

"the twelve names of the twelve apostles of the Lamb",[3] and their names are inscribed there precisely because the apostles followed the Lamb to his destiny.

The source of the disciples' life and guidance is the sacrificial Lamb who was slain, and his followers go to Life by sharing his own sacrificial destiny. If the life of the Lamb can be communicated to the world through the Lamb's followers, it is because these perpetuate in the world, in their own flesh, the Passion and Resurrection of the Lamb of God. What they are learning at bottom by following Jesus is how to die to themselves so as to live as new creatures in Christ. In our own life, too, all our praying and doing should be ordered to a continual act of self-sacrifice in union with Jesus' redemptive death.

If Jesus reveals the Father to us and this revelation is our salvation; if Jesus is permanently the obedient, meek, and humble Son; and if Jesus does indeed give us rest, but only on condition that we willingly subject our neck to his yoke—*subjugate* ourselves to him, literally—we may well then ask how it is that this process occurs, the process that turns us into his *disciples*. What concrete means does Jesus use to work these radical changes in our person, changes that frighten us at first but that step by step lead us to true joy in our soul?

Before we go into our text, we should first briefly consider how we should approach this and all the other Gospel passages in which we shall seek the meaning of

[3] Rev 21:14.

discipleship. The *Catechism of the Catholic Church* opens
with the following words: "Father, . . . this is eternal
life, that they may know you, the only true God, and
Jesus Christ whom you have sent."[4] In this context the
verb "to know" obviously refers, not to the acquisition
of facts or ideas, but to progressive admission into the
intimacy of the person of the Father, analogous to the
way in which people love one another as a result of long
association. "No one has ever seen God", writes Saint
John in his Prologue; "the only Son, who is in the bosom of the Father, he has made him known."[5] If the life
of our soul, our very "salvation", consists in knowing
God intimately as source of our being, it is also true that
only in the Son will we come to know God. In other
words, *Jesus is the living exegesis of the Father*, as the Greek
text of this verse of John affirms quite literally. The disciples' association with Jesus within time would then be
modeled on the pattern of the incarnate Word's own association with the Father in eternity. Therefore, just as
Jesus says of himself, "The Son can do nothing of his
own accord, but only what he sees the Father doing",[6]
so, too, does he say of his disciples, "I have given you an
example, that you also should do as I have done to you."[7]
And Peter, for his part, exclaims in the presence of the
Sanhedrin: "We cannot but speak of what we have seen

[4] Jn 17:3.
[5] Jn 1:18.
[6] Jn 5:19.
[7] Jn 13:15.

and heard."[8] Christ's presence among us, his disciples, is truly an opening up and an extension within us creatures of the eternal relationship of love between the Father and the Son in the Holy Spirit. The Christian community is thus a visible manifestation of the divine life of the Holy Trinity, and the Church—the Body of Christ—is consequently the place where the vital knowledge that saves is communicated.

Let us now read our text, paying close attention to every detail, since in the Gospel nothing is superfluous:

> Now when Jesus saw great crowds around him, he gave orders to go over to the other side. And a scribe came up and said to him, "Teacher, I will follow you wherever you go." And Jesus said to him, "Foxes have holes, and birds of the air have nests; but the Son of man has nowhere to lay his head." Another of the disciples said to him, "Lord, let me first go and bury my father." But Jesus said to him, "Follow me, and leave the dead to bury their own dead."
>
> And when he got into the boat, his disciples followed him. And behold, there arose a great storm on the sea, so that the boat was being swamped by the waves; but he was asleep. And they went and woke him, saying, "Save, Lord; we are perishing." And he said to them, "Why are you afraid, O men of little faith?" Then he rose and rebuked the winds and the sea; and there was a great calm. And the men marveled, saying, "What sort of man is this, that even winds and sea obey him?"[9]

[8] Acts 4:20.
[9] Mt 8:18–27.

The general structure of the event is a movement away from an initial shore; secondly, the experience of sailing on a lake; and, finally, the landing on the other shore. This is clearly the structure of a rite of passage, an initiation to new experiences that make the disciples to be a unique group set apart from the crowds by their abiding in Jesus' company. They are persons whom Jesus forms personally, with his own hands, we might say, according to his Heart. The disciples do not know what is happening or where they are going or why. They know only that they are with Jesus and that obeying him is a good thing even though they do not understand his motives. They do not choose a separate destiny of their own but find their joy in sharing Jesus' destiny. It is enough for them to know that Jesus has not thus far disappointed them or led them astray and that he exudes a mysterious aura of wisdom, of always knowing what he is about. As for the disciples, they must live by faith even though they are following a mentor who is quite visible.

The scene also clearly evokes the Exodus and the crossing of the Red Sea. Here, too, firm land had to be left behind for the uncertainty of water, and the Jews had to trust God's words through Moses telling them that only along this path lay the way to salvation. By leaving the land behind, the disciples are also leaving behind all their old ideas, habits, desires, and prejudices, and they abandon themselves into Jesus' hands and better judgment. The water symbolizes the danger of the unknown, the threat of the uncertain. In the Old Testament, great monsters symbolic of evil were thought to dwell in the deep waters, so that, as far as the disciples are concerned, they are here sailing right over the heads of evil forces.

Jesus is presently staging a deliberate spiritual showdown by exposing the disciples to their own deepest fears. The image is baptismal, since in baptism above all we experience the death of the old man and the birth of the new. Water must first kill if it is to give new life, and, even though we qualify this death with words like "symbolic" and "spiritual", nevertheless death is still death and cannot feel like anything else. Sins must be drowned, as well as the tendency to sin, an inclination aided and abetted by the chaos normally reigning in our passions. In the place of such chaos must be born the saving virtues: trust, faith, hope, the ability to love. The crossing of the lake, then, symbolizes the deepest possible transformation of the persons involved. At this point the disciples surely know nothing of any "glorious future", and, like the Jews at the Exodus, they are probably mumbling in their hearts: "Next time, Lord, please do someone *else* the favor of election!"

But note that Jesus is not here a mere intermediary or instrument of God, as Moses had been at the Red Sea. Nowhere does he consult God; rather, he consistently acts on his own. He reveals the Father, not from the distance and second-hand, but in his own being, words, and actions. As divine Word incarnate, he has no need for an external dialogue with God in order to seek inspiration and effective words or divine orders to be carried out.

Jesus acts as if he himself were God, present and visible. Only this explains why the disciples—feeling this divine presence and attraction in Jesus, their teacher and friend —follow him blindly without understanding the whys, hows, and wheres, despite all the difficulties involved. They only know that, being with Jesus, they cannot go wrong, regardless of how contradictory and deeply unsettling many things may appear to them to be.

Even while still on land, Jesus begins acting in a disconcerting fashion. The Master's strange attitude anticipates, at the level of the emotions, the impending threat of the waves, and this shows how he is deliberately orchestrating the event as he uses the lake for his own purposes. On the one hand, he takes the initiative of separating his own followers from the crowds, and they are quite conscious that such election bespeaks privilege and special affection. On the other hand, he gives a truly shocking reply to the scribe who volunteers to join the group. Jesus roughly, almost rudely, corrects the facileness of the scribe's generous offer, "I will follow you wherever you go." Indeed, how easy it is to be enthusiastic and generous while we are still on firm land! We imagine that Jesus will provide nothing but assurances and comforting camaraderie. The great irony is that Jesus' divine being as Son of God makes of him the poorest and most naked of men. Foxes and birds have more material security and stability than he, who does not even have a place to lay his head. The very one who can give rest to our souls does not himself have any resting place in this world! This is because all his security and profound stability come to him, not from the world, but from the Father. As Saint John tells us, the only place where the Son may rest is in the bosom (*kolpos*, Jn 1:18) of the Father, which makes him simultaneously utterly divine by nature and utterly destitute in this world. In our world, God is a vagrant.

Thus, if Jesus deliberately disconcerts the scribe, seeming to reject him as disciple, it is precisely because he wants to teach us unequivocally that we, too, have to draw ever closer to the Father's bosom as our sole resting place, and the condition for this is detachment from all worldly and human security. We cannot have it both ways. To the scribe Jesus seems to say: "You really want to follow me everywhere? Do you even vaguely realize what that means and who it is you want to follow? Do you know I am a Lamb who is on his way to being slain and that my business is to redeem the world with my blood?" The Christian life, above all the unconditional following of Jesus in the contemplative life, is either a humble reënactment on a daily basis of Jesus' Passion and Resurrection, or it is a sham. Paradoxically, a contemplative's vow of "stability" means that that person can never settle down in ease and comfort, since the contemplative's place of rest can only be Jesus' self-sacrificing Heart, enshrined within the bosom (*kolpos*) on which John rested (Jn 13:23).

To the other disciple Jesus gives an even more shocking answer, since he appears almost to be inciting him to violate the Fourth Commandment. But the father that the disciple wants to bury is already dead, so the corpse becomes an obvious symbol of the way in which a disciple must regard everything he has left behind from his standpoint at Jesus' side: Compared to the person of Jesus, everything else is as if it were dead. But Jesus is all the while building a new form of family, the Church, the great brotherhood and sisterhood that has God as Father, and before this reality even one's human family takes second place. This surely does not mean, however, that we must suddenly live like angels in a wholly spiritualized world, without any use of material possessions and without feeling human affections. Not at all, for God has created us with bodies and as social beings. Nevertheless, in the order of the affections and loves of our soul, we must strive for the day when we can truly say that the love of God and the desire to do his holy will are our deepest motivation. As Christians, we may not love even our own family more than God and his unfathomable will, and at times very painful sacrifices are required of us if we are to live this truth. After all, for the sake of our redemption the Son himself had to let go of the glory of equality with the Father, and for love of the world the Father abandoned the Son to the Cross.

At last we find ourselves aboard ship, floating on the waters of a vast lake. The Lake of Genesareth is so vast and deep that it is usually called a "sea". It is famous for its very violent and sudden storms. No sooner is the little crew out over the deep than one of these storms begins attacking the boat, so much so that it "was being swamped by the waves". As we have said, we suspect that Jesus put his disciples on this boat with clear knowledge that such a storm would break out. For mysterious reasons of his own, Jesus wanted to expose his friends to mortal fear. He wanted to teach them things essential to faith, things that can be learned only in this way, by suffering them in one's own flesh. We have here an obvious instance of the Word being a scalpel that intervenes in our sick being so as to heal it. Jesus is probing the souls of his disciples in order to ascertain to what point fear and distrust need to be excised so that joy and trust in him and in his Father may begin to grow.

The disciples may now ask themselves to what extent they have been following Jesus out of mere curiosity, out of boredom with their dull lives, out of discontent and restlessness, or simply in order to associate with someone wise and important. Or, on the other hand, to what extent do they follow him because they recognize in him the Messiah who has come to redeem Israel and the world. Only the exposure to mortal danger will tell.

And, in the midst of the storm, Jesus *sleeps*. Jesus pretends not to realize, pretends to be indifferent, unconcerned. And yet, there he is in the same boat with them, very much a man undergoing the same storm. What a marvelous image of what our own trust in God should be, thus to sleep in a raging storm! Here we see clearly that "trust" is no abstract mental virtue, but a radical act of *self-entrustment*, of depositing one's being into the hands of God precisely when, humanly speaking, the circum-

stances would seem to call for the greatest self-initiative
and self-management. Remember Jesus' prayer on the
Cross: "Father, into your hands I commit my spirit!"[10]
This storm anticipates the cataclysm of Calvary, but in a
more didactic mode that still admits dialogue. At Calvary
Jesus would be wholly engulfed by the waves of suffering.

Regardless of how harassed and perturbed we might be
by all life's crises, why can we not, like Jesus, have our
soul at rest, anchored in God's good pleasure? This is the
rest that Jesus wants us to partake of, the rest that comes
from having taken up obedience and filial love toward
the Father as our primary occupation. If we only knew
how possible this is! If we admit Christ into the boat of
our life for him to sail with us, even the most tormented
moments at the surface of the emotions can coexist with
a deep calm, the deep sleep of a will that rests, like Jesus,
in the bosom of the eternal Father. In any event, is there
any other hope for us? While the Son of Man cannot rest
in material nests and lairs like the birds and the foxes, he
finds his rest paradoxically on the high seas of divine obedience and adventure! We must strive to find a happiness
that does not vanish every time a tragedy, or even a mild
reversal in our expectations, occurs. We cannot surrender our souls as hostages to the whims of this world's
waves, to float upon them like helpless corks. Jesus offers us a happiness and a joy grounded in trust in his

[10] Lk 23:46 = Ps 30:5.

Father and in the faith that, despite appearances to the contrary, he really is there with us, although his manner may be silent and discreet, there watching over our welfare and guiding our path toward "the other shore", the Kingdom of Heaven. The stakes are high, and the price in self-surrendering trust utterly worth paying.

Fear then wrenches from the disciples a plea that is more like a primal cry of the soul: "Save, Lord; we are perishing." Would the scribe be glad at this moment that he had followed Jesus "everywhere", even into the heart of this storm? Is not this moment of literally abysmal fear precisely what Jesus had warned him against? And yet does not our heart leap with joy at realizing that even this harrowing situation has been anticipated by Jesus and is therefore already enfolded within his wisdom and providence? He proves this by his presence, for he does not send us alone into the storm. By sheer force of fear for their lives, the disciples are learning their total dependency on God. They are learning how to be God's children in the same way that Jesus is Son. They are gauging what they still lack of faith and trust precisely at the moment when they have to begin trusting because they have no other recourse and because their own emotional and practical capacities have been reduced to nil.

And so, when Jesus rebukes them even before he rebukes the waves, they already know to what he is referring. Jesus gets his own cherished friends into straits so that they will learn what it means to believe and to trust. We simply cannot learn trust while all the time ensconced in natural security. His relationship with them, and their relationship with the Father of love and dependency in and through Jesus, must henceforth be the unshakable foundation beneath every trial, revolution, reversal, tempest, and tragedy that occurs in the world.

Once the disciples have run out of every possible personal resource of strength and understanding, once mortal fear has washed their eyes clean, *then* and only then does the Lord work the marvel: by a mere word, he calms the winds and the sea. In a real sense, Jesus can do this in my life only when I allow him and beg him to, only when I run to him with untiring pleas and thus show him that I no longer trust in myself, only when I stop playing sorcerer's apprentice over the cauldron of my life and become silent, expectant disciple. I have to allow him to be the Lord of the tormented sea of my soul, the Lord of the waves of my passions—Lord of both my greed and my sadness (for sadness can be a vice), Lord of both my anger and my eroticism, my envy, my pride, my drive to accomplish and shine and be admired.

The result of this whole episode is that the disciples begin to understand that "the waves cannot drown those who are borne—not by their own will and understanding—but by the Spirit of God", because this Spirit lends wings to the soul while our own devices are burdens that make us sink.[11] And, even though they already know

---

[11] Antiphon for Lauds on the Benedictine feast of Saints Maur and Placid (January 15).

Jesus in many respects, this crisis on the lake forces them to ask themselves what is perhaps the most important question we, too, could ever ask ourselves: "Who is this man, that even the winds and the sea obey him?"

Let us, too, allow this question to enjoy an unending echo in our hearts, and may its reverberation little by little transform our lives.

4

LEAPING BARTIMÆUS

W E UNDERTAKE yet another step in the process of becoming Jesus' disciples. Let us remember never to avert our gaze from Jesus and always to direct all our attention to the smallest detail of his conduct, words, gestures, and silences in the Gospel text, looking here for the revelation of the Father and the intentions of his Heart, trying to discover what he wants to do with us and what he wants from us, for the glory of God and the world's salvation.

It is ironical that we should be speaking of gazing and looking intently to introduce a meditation based on the experience of a blind man. The episode of the blind man of Jericho is located in Mark just before the triumphal entry into Jerusalem, and hence it is a threshold to Holy Week and the events of the Passion. It is the last miracle of Jesus in Mark, and it thus carries considerable symbolic importance, as if it were a summary of all Jesus' active ministry. Giving sight to a blind man is a perfect image of what Jesus wants to operate in us: to open the eyes of our soul to the vision of faith—the vision of who he is, of how he reveals the Father, and of what destiny he intends for us.

This central section of the Gospel of Mark had begun

with the healing of the other blind man, the one of Bethsaida (8:22–26). You may recall him as the one who had first seen people in a blurred manner, "like walking trees". The healing at Bethsaida is immediately followed by Peter's confession, which proclaims Jesus as the Christ, the Messiah anointed by God. The whole section tells of the slow pilgrimage of Jesus and his disciples from Galilee in the north toward Jerusalem in the south, where Jesus will be judged and condemned. Jesus uses the pilgrimage as a school through which to initiate his disciples to the most intimate secrets of his Heart. The healing of two blind men is thus the beginning and the conclusion of the whole section, as if to make us understand that all Jesus' miracles and teachings intend the revelation of the truth of who he is and how he works redemption.

But to apprehend these truths we first need to be healed of the illness of worldly vision. Our main problem is that we think we already see, whereas in truth we are blind. Bartimæus is most fortunate in realizing the precise nature of what ails him. Together with Peter we have to learn to see and recognize in Jesus the one and only Redeemer, the beloved Son whom God sends to win us over to his friendship and fidelity. "Who do you say that I am?"[1] Jesus asks Peter, and the question is almost identical to the one the disciples asked themselves on the lake: "What sort of man is this, that even winds and sea obey him?"[2] And, in the present context, we may ask:

[1] Mk 8:29.
[2] Mt 8:27.

"Who is this, who has the power of giving sight to blind persons with his mere word?"

Once again, let us put ourselves in the position of the disciples, following Jesus everywhere he goes and learning from him what is compassion and what is the power of God in our midst. Let us learn above all that the first thing we have to admit is our own blindness. We may not be blind in our body; but we are surely blind in our soul, and like the disciples we have to submit to this pilgrimage, following Jesus incessantly, so that he, by means of his healing presence, can enlighten the eyes of our heart and enable us to contemplate him as he is. Let us remember Saint Paul's beautiful words in 2 Corinthians:

> We all, with unveiled face, beholding the glory of the Lord, are being changed into his likeness from one degree of glory to another; for this comes from the Lord who is the Spirit. . . . Our gospel is veiled . . . only to those who are perishing. In their case the god of this world has blinded the minds of the unbelievers, to keep them from seeing the light of the gospel of the glory of Christ, who is the likeness of God. . . . For it is the God who said, "Let light shine out of darkness," who has shone in our hearts to give the light of the knowledge of the glory of God in the face of Christ.[3]

We could reflect for a long time on this beautiful text, so rich in spiritual doctrine. But I will stress only one of its themes: that Jesus Christ is the visible image of the

[3] 2 Cor 3:18; 4:3-4, 6.

invisible God of glory; that the eternal splendor of God's glory shines *from* the face of Jesus, most piercingly at Tabor and at the Resurrection, and that the eyes of faith can indeed see this marvelous light. As a result of persevering lovingly in the contemplation of Jesus' resplendent Face by praying and meditating on the Gospel, we ourselves will gradually be transformed into what our eyes contemplate. Thus, we, too, become the image of God, radiating God's glory, truth, and love into this world that so desperately needs it.

We now contemplate in detail the beautiful Face of Jesus in this episode of the blind Bartimæus, gladly submitting ourselves as disciples to what Jesus wants to teach us by his words but above all by his resplendent presence:

> As he was leaving Jericho with his disciples and a great multitude, Bartimæus, a blind beggar, the son of Timæus, was sitting by the roadside. And when he heard that it was Jesus of Nazareth, he began to cry out and say, "Jesus, Son of David, have mercy on me!" And many rebuked him, telling him to be silent; but he cried out all the more, "Son of David, have mercy on me!" And Jesus stopped and said, "Call him." And they called the blind man, saying to him, "Take heart; rise, he is calling you." And throwing off his mantle he sprang up and came to Jesus. And Jesus said to him, "What do you want me to do for you?" And the blind man said to him, "Master, let me receive my sight." And Jesus said to him, "Go your way; your faith has made you well." And immediately he received his sight and followed him on the way.[4]

[4] Mk 10:46–52.

Jesus and his disciples have just exited Jericho, a very ancient city near Jerusalem. It is the last stop before the triumphal entry into Jerusalem on Palm Sunday. A huge crowd is pressing around Jesus, in addition to the disciples. But Jesus has no interest in faceless crowds, only in needy individuals. The disciples assume that only they are Jesus' chosen ones, and even among themselves they argue about rank. Just a moment before, those intrepid and rather foolish brothers James and John had asked Jesus for the privilege of sitting one at his right and the other at his left in the glory of the Kingdom.[5] What the disciples are about to learn is how to be true disciples, and the sobering thing is that it is not one of their number who is going to set the example. Rather, it is the blind beggar seated at the side of the road.

Let us follow the episode step by step. We can identify no less than six distinct moments in this encounter, each of them offering rich insights into the mystery of our own life in Christ.

1. In contrast to all those crowding and pushing around Jesus, the blind man is alone, apart, sunken in his misery. No one knows more than he how needy he is, how helpless he is left to himself. This alone shows us the first absolute condition for being a disciple: not to deceive ourselves, fully to acknowledge our interior state, to see ourselves reduced to misery after having attempted to create for ourselves a life without God or one in which we pay only lip service to God, a life in which,

---

[5] Cf. Mk 10:37.

de facto even if not in theory, we are our own lord and master. Every human being, if honest, should recognize himself in this blind beggar, Bartimæus. He is totally dependent on God and neighbor in taking even one step or putting a bite of food in his mouth. But his misery is not lacking in intelligence. Notice where he has stationed himself: at the side of the road where everyone passes by. He has not stayed shut away in his home in some dark corner feeling sorry for himself and waiting for God to send him a miraculous angel to help him. He has come out of himself and exposed his misery to the world's stream of life and to God.

2. It seems he was not looking only for human compassion, but for the Kingdom of God as well. For, "when he heard that it was Jesus of Nazareth [going by], he began to *cry out* and say, 'Jesus, Son of David, have mercy on me!' "[6] Beyond all the little alms that kept him going from day to day, it seems he was searching for the Redeemer of Israel, since simply at hearing the name of Jesus of Nazareth he at once begins shouting to him, invoking him with the messianic title "Son of David". From the midst of his misery, he recognizes who Jesus truly is much more clearly than anyone else present, including the official disciples. And his profession of faith in Jesus' messianic identity is not merely intellectual, since the blind man becomes hoarse proclaiming it to the whole universe in a plea that implores Jesus' compassion. The

[6] Emphasis mine.

man is making a public act of worship. Shouting, he tries to compensate for what his eyes cannot see and for the road his feet cannot find. Through that shout, repeated more and more loudly, he pours out his whole soul into Jesus' ears. Bartimæus sees only with the eyes of his heart what the eyes of his body cannot see, and thus he sees more deeply than all others. He does not ask for money, food, lodging, or clothing—all of which would be a merely partial and passing relief in his suffering. His very misery has made him bolder: what he demands through his shouting is the compassion of the Son of God. He demands that all of God's goodness may pour out upon himself and his ailment.

We too have to *recognize* ourselves as truly needy in order then to *expose* ourselves in this way to God's transforming action in Jesus and to *dare* to persist against whatever obstacles may arise, coming from within ourselves or from others or from adverse circumstances. Nothing and no one would separate this blind man from the Redeemer he had so longed for and who finally on this day passed by where he was seated. God is faithful, and in the end he always comes to those who await him with such longing, for surely Bartimæus' shouting expressed a long-standing thirst for salvation. Here, then, the blind beggar is teaching us three essential stages of discipleship: first, the recognition of one's true condition; second, the exposition of it to the one who can heal; finally, the persistence required in the face of opposition.

3. Jesus hears his name being shouted by the blind

man over the tumult of the crowd and over the objec-
tions of those who had tried to silence him. Do I have
the boldness of Bartimæus, or am I instead ruled by different forms of timidity, shame, bad conscience, fatalism,
or even thinly veiled despair that makes me stifle the ardent plea that my heart, in its visceral wisdom, wants
to hurl at Jesus? We Christians must implore our Father
with all the boldness and daring of the child who knows
that nothing can be denied us by the God who loves us
and who is the Lord of heaven and earth. This is the
virtue Saint Paul calls *parrhêsia*, the freedom of speech
and the bold trust that is our baptismal birthright as co-
heirs of Christ. Jesus is always listening—listening to see
if he hears our deepest voice rising above the tumult of
the world and of our passions, our voice unremittingly
shouting his holy Name, shouting for him to come and
help us.

And he never fails to respond: "Jesus stopped and said,
'Call him.'" Jesus contradicts his disciples, who want to
keep the blind man far away from their teacher. He orders the disciples to bring Bartimæus to him. The true
disciple does not follow his own hunches as to what is
appropriate or not in the apostolate. We must be rid of
a purely human prudence that keeps God's dearest creature, man, separated from God through human respect
for appearances and socio-religious conventions. The disciples do not think that a blind beggar is worth their
teacher's time; but Jesus does. Perhaps Jesus, himself a
poor man not having anywhere to lay his head, identi-

fies with the blind beggar just as he identifies with little
infants, and so he wants to be where the blind man is
just as much as the blind man wants to be where he is.

The disciples are ordered to extend, to one they consider unworthy of it, the call they themselves first received. The sole task of those who have been called *by*
Jesus, it would appear, is to call *to* Jesus; they will thus be
furthering their own privilege and vocation. Like Jesus,
who has generously surrendered "the form of God", the
disciples must learn not to make their discipleship something to clutch greedily. This portion of our passage is
highly instructive in teaching us the best use we can make
of our voices in this world: With Jesus, we are to encour-
age and heal; with the disciples, we are to call others
to Jesus; and, with Bartimæus, we are to implore Jesus
boldly and unceasingly.

4. When he hears that Jesus is calling him, the blind
man reacts in a very moving and revealing way: "Throwing off his mantle he sprang up and came to Jesus." What
energy of faith! His dire need is energized by the call; a
little resurrection then occurs. This man is not going to
waste a single instant in responding to Jesus' call. We can
feel the throbbing of his joy and enthusiasm. After having waited for so long, finally his hour arrives to be sum-
moned before the person of the Lord. His own skin can
barely contain him. The gesture of throwing off the mantle expresses a hundred things at once: he wants to go
as lightly as possible toward Jesus, without any more en-
cumbrances; he wants to leave behind his old life and his

misery, symbolized by those rags; he no longer wants to
conceal his shame and his need, but wants to expose himself naked before Jesus' loving and transforming gaze. . . .
From Jesus he wants to hide nothing. The more naked
and needy, the more jubilant he is, because his contact
with Jesus will be the more intimate, and this ecstatic
jubilation makes him *spring up* like a rocket. He does not
lose a single instant giving himself cosmetic touches, un-
like us, who spend much too much time before the interior mirror of vanity, wanting to present even to God
a touched-up version of ourselves. Bartimæus wants to
come before Jesus just as he is, because he knows that
God loves, not our illusions about ourselves or our self-
constructed images, but the "me" he has created and only
that, even if I myself do not approve of it.

5. If the blind man can respond without hesitation to
the question Jesus asks of him, it is because he knows
himself well and has learned how to distinguish between
his true needs and all those frivolous desires that deceive
us. "What do you want me to do for you?"—"Master,
let me receive my sight." Jesus, of course, already real-
izes what is the nature of his problem; but he wants to
hear it from the man's own lips. It is possible that another
person, having grown used to being blind, would have
asked for riches, fame, pleasures, or power—or for all of
these things *and his sight besides*. But, like Solomon in his
famous prayer for wisdom, the blind man limits himself
to the essential thing he needs in order to be a whole human being, and by asking Jesus for it he makes an implicit

act of faith in Jesus' ability to heal his blindness. The Son of David, he knows, has not come to liberate Israel from the Romans or to establish an earthly kingdom or to fulfill our every whim: he has come to restore the whole of our humanity to what God had made it in the beginning and, in particular, to give us the organs necessary for us to see him and the glory of his Kingdom, to see the divine light of the Father reflected, as Saint Paul says, on the Face of the Son.

It is crucial that Jesus says to the man: "Your faith has saved you." Why does Jesus not say, instead, something like "The power of God has saved you through me who am his incarnate compassion"? Because God's love and power finds itself with its hands tied, so to speak, where it does not find faith, where it does not find a heart that recognizes who Jesus is and invokes him with all its strength that he may intervene and change its life. We have to invite Jesus continually to become Lord of our life. He never imposes himself by force because, being Love, he wants to be loved in return, and love is born only from freedom and never from force or obligation. What is true at the natural level is also true at the supernatural. God cannot force us to love him. Yet, instead of loving God unconditionally, we spend most of our time piously trying to manipulate his power to suit our own desires: we want to have God at our beck and call. The faith that saves, then, is the unity or embrace that results from God's desire and power to save us meeting our own desire and need to be saved by him. Only those are saved

who want to be saved, those who direct their steps toward the One who alone can work this miracle—and salvation is, after all, the chief of God's miracles, the only
one that ultimately matters, and every specific healing is
but a sign of the miracle of salvation. We have to place
ourselves, voluntarily and gratefully, in the hands of the
Physician of bodies and souls, confidently manifesting to
him our every illness and complaint.

6. Our episode concludes in a way that is no less surprising than everything else we have seen. The blind man
of Bethsaida had been sent home by Jesus after being
healed. Bartimæus is different. When Jesus says to him,
"Go your way; your faith has made you well", he recovers his sight instantaneously. And the first thing upon
which he naturally fixes his brand-new eyes to break
them in, so to speak, is the Face of Jesus, his Savior. It is
in order to see Jesus, the visible image of God, more than
anything else, that Bartimæus recovers his sight. And I
think that at once he falls in love with the beauty of Jesus'
goodness, made burning and piercing by the divine light
emanating from Jesus' eyes. Is this mere romantic fanta-
sizing? I think not, because when Jesus says to him, literally, "Go away! [*hypagê*]", without a second's hesitation
he "followed [Jesus] on the way".

Jesus gives him his freedom, the option of doing whatever he chooses with the great gift of grace just received.
Jesus actually puts one last test in the man's path by thus
dismissing him. But what this man, in his great nobility of
soul, chooses to do is to cling permanently to following

Jesus on *Jesus'* way. For Bartimæus, seeing is henceforth one and the same as seeing Jesus, and seeing Jesus is one and the same as following Jesus on his way. Bartimæus has allowed Jesus' presence, call of him, encouragement, and act of healing to effect a convergence of the roads of their two lives. Not a stupid or ungrateful man, this Bartimæus, thus to abandon himself so completely into the hands and destiny of the one who has just revealed himself to him as the source of light and salvation. One is not "saved" only to continue living autonomously, as before. Bartimæus no longer wishes for his life to follow any way different from that of Jesus. Such joyful relinquishing of independence bestows extraordinary spiritual energy and vitality, because it connects one with the source of divine power.

But did the formerly blind man know that this way led to Jerusalem and Calvary, and, if he had known, would it have mattered?

After witnessing such a scene, what should we not be willing to give up in order to become this blind man, or at least to have a little of his humility, frankness, self-knowledge, boldness, persistence, enthusiasm, energy, and, above all, his trust in the Lord? Truly, Jesus has ravished his heart.

Let us pray that our own miseries and blindnesses, all the apparent dead ends of our lives, once exposed patiently and thoroughly to God's mercy in Jesus, may become occasions of loving surrender and may, therefore, yield such fruits as these in our lives. But remember that this requires an ability to pray continuously with great concentration and energy; and, since we have only a limited supply of attention, we will be too weak and scattered to pray as we ought if we habitually squander our spiritual energy in other directions. We may say that the wise practice of "energy conservation" is essential to a vibrant spiritual life, so that our whole soul may be spent in Bartimæus' one cry: "Jesus, Son of David, have mercy on me!"

5

THE NECESSARY
WASTEFULNESS OF LOVE

O NE OF THE MAIN THEMES of the Gospel of Luke is
surely the joy and thanksgiving that well up in our
hearts at discovering the mercy of God, especially when
in his compassion he forgives our sins. This forgiveness,
inseparable from our own repentance, is the beginning
of a new life, one in which all our old values and attitudes must change completely. If, before, we have lived
for ourselves—our pleasure, success, survival, really not
much better than the lowest microscopic organisms—
from now on we shall live for Another: our focus in life
will be outward, toward others, similar to God's own
outward-looking focus as Creator and Redeemer. How
will this change take place in us? This change will occur when we begin to be disciples of Jesus and when
we rejoice more in his beauty and goodness than in our
own myriad desires, as ephemeral as they are stingy and
greedy.

We recall once again that God's beauty and goodness, reflected on the Face of Jesus, may be beheld only
by those who first see themselves as the sinners and
wounded souls they truly are, like the admirable woman
in Luke we will now see. The way toward the contem-

plation of God's beauty begins with the recognition of one's own deformity and ugliness, that is, of our need to be re-created, reformed, made beautiful in our soul by loving contact with the Father's incarnate love, Jesus of Nazareth.

Let us now read our text:

One of the Pharisees asked [Jesus] to eat with him, and he went into the Pharisee's house, and sat at table. And behold, a woman of the city, who was a sinner, when she learned that he was sitting at table in the Pharisee's house, brought an alabaster flask of ointment, and standing behind him at his feet, weeping, she began to wet his feet with her tears, and wiped them with the hair of her head, and kissed his feet, and anointed them with the ointment. Now when the Pharisee who had invited him saw it, he said to himself, "If this man were a prophet, he would have known who and what sort of woman this is who is touching him, for she is a sinner." And Jesus answering said to him, "Simon, I have something to say to you." And he answered, "What is it, Teacher?" "A certain creditor had two debtors; one owed five hundred denarii, and the other fifty. When they could not pay, he forgave them both. Now which of them will love him more?" Simon answered, "The one, I suppose, to whom he forgave more." And he said to him, "You have judged rightly." Then turning toward the woman he said to Simon, "Do you see this woman? I entered your house, you gave me no water for my feet, but she has wet my feet with her tears and wiped them with her hair. You gave me no kiss, but from the time I came in she has not ceased to kiss my feet. You did not anoint my head with oil, but she has anointed my feet with ointment. Therefore I tell you, her sins, which are many, are forgiven, for she loved much; but he who is forgiven little, loves little." And he said to her, "Your sins are forgiven." Then those who were at table with him began to say among themselves, "Who is this, who even forgives sins?" And he said to the woman, "Your faith has saved you; go in peace."[1]

The power of the story derives in large part from the extreme contrast it makes between the attitude of Simon the Pharisee and that of the sinful woman. Simon's attitude powerfully puts in relief the way in which the woman sees herself. Simon seems to hold a few very clear and very simple religious principles; but this is a harmful simplicity and a deceptive piety that sees the world as statically divided into good people and sinful people. The good are those who keep their obligations; the sinners are those who commit flagrant faults. God loves the good; God does not love sinners; in fact, God distances himself from sinners. Simon is good; hence Simon distances himself from sinners. Jesus does not distance himself from the sinful woman; hence Jesus is not being led by God's Spirit . . .

The strange thing, however, is that the all-holy and all-pure God does not happen to think like Simon. Only God is good, as God himself is the first to know, and, therefore, he does not define the good and the sinful as

[1] Lk 7:36–50.

Simon does, but rather wants to forgive all. If we are good, it is by participating in the divine goodness and not because we can be the source of our own goodness. And, besides, we can never be absolutely good, but only defectively so. So God does not weigh our good and evil actions on a scale in order to see which weigh more; that would be a child's game. God lives with the fact that most of us seem to need time to taste both good and evil, in order to mature in our final decision for the good. If God allows us to sin, it is for us to learn how easily we tend toward evil and that our only hope lies in him. This is why God can so easily forget our sins and personal chaos, provided that through them or despite them we arrive at true love.

Why had Simon invited Jesus to his home, only to treat him as he does? Did he want to exploit his reputation as teacher? Did he want to boast that someone important had eaten at his house? Did he want to feel proud of himself, because, if this reputedly holy man accepted his invitation, this clearly proclaimed Simon's own sanctity and purity? What are our own reasons for desiring an association with Jesus? An enhanced public image, for others to say, "Look at how religious he is, quite the little saint already"? To be admired as being better than others in the eyes of God? Life and grace will surely shatter such illusions quickly. The fact remains that Simon had no passion for Jesus whatsoever. He appears to have been a calculator who exploited social and religious situations for his own self-advancement and vainglory. He did not even offer Jesus the minimum of courtesy required by Middle Eastern customs. He only wanted to be able to say afterward: "The famous rabbi ate at my house." He was, in other words, a spiritual mercenary, seeking to profit from Jesus' presence. Simon had no wish whatsoever for Jesus to transform his life; he merely wanted to use Jesus to canonize his own conceit.

By contrast, Jesus' mere presence in the town mysteriously draws the sinful woman to him, magnet-like, and how different are her motivations from those of the hypocritical Pharisee! While Simon wants to use Jesus to enhance his own public image as a pious and holy man, the woman for her part feels that the simple presence of Jesus' holiness in her proximity is an instant judgment that reveals all the ugliness of her sins. How truthful and bold she is in her self-appraisal! But, instead of going to hide like Adam and Eve at feeling so shamefully naked before the glance of the Son of God, penetrating miraculously through all the walls of the town to arrive at her own heart, what does she do?

The deep wisdom that grace infuses into her at that moment makes her *rush* immediately toward the one who, just by being present in her village, makes her feel the full sorrow for her sins. Like the apostles on the boat, like the blind man Bartimæus, this sinful woman knows that her only salvation lies in having recourse at once to the one who simultaneously judges her by virtue of his sanctity and forgives her by virtue of his immense mercy. In one moment of luminous intuition, this woman real-izes that Jesus is at once the destroyer of her sins, the victor over all evil, *and* the Bridegroom of her soul.

Two troparia from the Syriac tradition magnificently comment on the scene. The first ponders Jesus' motivation for going to the Pharisee's in the first place: "Who would not be taken with the mercy of Christ, who, in order to save the sinner, invites himself to Simon's house? For the sake of her who hungers for forgiveness, he himself wants to hunger for Simon's table." And the second troparion interprets for us the silent thoughts that the woman directs at Jesus: "It is you, my Lord, who desired that we should grasp you and implore you. For, if you had not wanted us to grasp you, you would not have become incarnate. It is you who called me to come near you. I saw your beauty and ran toward you."[2]

How impressive this woman who, despite the great emotions shaking her soul, does not utter a single word throughout the episode. Instead, she makes herself present to Jesus and performs actions directed exclusively at his person. She does not want to call any attention to herself, only to him. All the verbal dialogue takes place between Jesus and the Pharisee; what transpires between Jesus and the woman is the mute dialogue of love, in which only the gestures of the body and the expression of the eyes can communicate what is happening in the soul. Deep and overwhelming love is beyond words and arguments, beyond reason. The Pharisee's words have the effect of separating him from Jesus, of keeping Jesus far

[2] Syriac Liturgy for the feast of Saint Mary Magdalen.

from his soul, while the woman's silence unites her to Jesus as the surest bridge and bond. She has understood the full meaning of the injunction, "Be still, and know that I am God!"[3]

The woman's silence is rich in movements of the heart and symbolic actions that allow us to see what is occurring in her soul. Despite her rush to join Jesus, she does not come to him bereft of means to show him her love. Before coming to Simon's house, she buys "an alabaster flask of perfumed ointment". In the parallel episode in Mark,[4] we learn that this single flask of ointment, made of "spikenard", has an incredible value: "more than 300 denarii", which is to say the salary of almost a full year of work. This extravagant cost is explained by the fact that ointment of spikenard is an extract produced from a flower that grows only in the Himalaya mountains, which are both notoriously difficult to climb and very remote from Palestine. An ancient rabbinic tradition has it that the wonderfully fragrant spikenard was the only thing Adam and Eve were allowed to take with them when they were expelled from Eden after their sin. Its possession was to be for them a reminder of the joys that had been theirs in their original created state and, hence, also a reminder of the goodness and beauty of God and of his readiness to be reconciled to them and to reëstablish them in a condition of undiluted bliss.

It is astounding that the woman squanders such an amount of money in one great momentary gesture of

[3] Ps 46:10.
[4] Mk 14:3-9.

love, but even more astounding is the likelihood that, since she is probably a prostitute, surely the money with which she buys the ointment has been earned in a life of profitable sin. We may say, then, not only that she has repented of her many sins at feeling the proximity of Jesus' holiness, but that she shows this contrition by converting the fruit of her sin into an act of love and praise. This tainted fruit is the only thing she has to offer; but the fire of her love transforms the ugliness of sin into the beauty of adoration. *Conversion* is not here a casual word, since it implies that all of a person's vital energy, until now wasted and abusively exploited, is now converted, "recycled" if you will, transformed into an energy of love that unites to God; and such conversion occurs by virtue of Jesus' mere presence as catalyst.

The woman did not cease being fiery and passionate when converting to Jesus; conversion did not turn her into a neutral and apathetic being, a condition some imagine to be a requirement for "piety". Quite the contrary: all her former eroticism, dark and mercenary as it was, now is transformed into generous acts, which have not even lost a certain erotic fervor and yet concern themselves solely with the person of the one Beloved. This washing of feet with tears, this rubbing of hair on feet and covering of feet with kisses, this anointing of the Lord's feet with precious ointment: What does all of this manifest if not the loving frenzy that wants to wipe out the dirty offenses and cruel wounds that she feels her sins have inflicted on Jesus' body? The woman does homage to the all-too-human and tired feet that had brought the

Spouse to her all the way from the Father's bosom—the feet that would be pierced into immobility to atone for all her waywardness.

Perfumed ointment such as she has brought was used in antiquity, among other things, for healing wounds. After repentance for sin, and as an essential part of the process of conversion and reconciliation of the soul with God, comes the necessary reparation for the sins committed, which are seen as a personal offense against God, whose presence and holiness are utterly personalized and made palpable in the body of Jesus. As Walker Percy has said in perfect Louisiana slang, Catholic Christianity is a religion in which we can "grab a holt" of God.

Like the blind Bartimæus, who recognizes Jesus as the Messiah, and like the apostles, who marvel at Jesus' lordly power over the sea and the winds, this woman intuits that Jesus of Nazareth is God among us, God reclining and eating at our very table, in our own town, God come to meet us in the foundering boat of our lives, at the side of the road where we have spent so much time begging in vain. The only thing that explains why this woman exhibits all her heart's repentance precisely to Jesus is that she recognizes in him the presence of the God that her sins have offended, the God who alone can give her forgiveness in an embrace of love. And Jesus himself declares that the woman, in her sinfulness, is his personal debtor and that her abundance of love for him has more than repaid what she owed him on account of her sins.[5]

[5] Cf. Lk 7:41–42, 47.

Meanwhile, very far from this loving intuition, Simon spends his time disputing with Jesus: about a sinner touching him, about whether consequently Jesus does not make it even to the category of "good prophet", about whether Jesus is a "teacher" who does not really know his trade very well . . . What probably worries Simon most is his own reputation: for this woman, by coming to Jesus while he is Simon's guest, has openly contaminated Simon's home and his table with her sins. Simon, who believes himself just, puts many conditions on God, thereby limiting and in a sense "caging" God's mercy by not allowing God to act in a manner contrary to Simon's own most ungenerous and prejudiced ideas, which stem from his concern for worldly religious respectability. The woman, by contrast, far from putting limits on God, wants only to pour out her whole being into the sea of divine mercy, there to drown all her sins and experience rebirth through this act of total self-surrender to a new life. She wants to destroy all the barriers that exist between herself and Jesus, in order to come to be but one thing with him, as Saint Paul says: "For to me to live is Christ."[6]

Which of these two shall we be, you and I: the "pious" Pharisee with the prejudiced soul, or this woman who has found the secret of how to convert the coal of sin into the diamond of love, by the sheer pressure of her desire and the heat of her devotion? In her reckless love,

[6] Phil 1:21.

she does not fear making a spectacle of herself by appearing in public breathless, all tears and disheveled hair.

Indeed, "her sins, which are many, are forgiven, for she loved much; but he who is forgiven little, loves little." Repentance triggered by the presence of Jesus, God's love in our lives; feelings and acts of reparation nourished by the love that impels us; forgiveness received from God: we have before us here the perfect structure of the process of conversion and reconciliation without which we cannot be disciples.

The fact that the woman expresses her contrition by acts of love squandered on the person of Jesus—uselessly, for the sheer joy of it—shows, in the first place, that actions are more eloquent than words because they give proof of truth in the soul. But, at an even deeper level, this shows that Christian conversion is not only a change of mind, a resolution like those vague ones we make at New Year's to improve our conduct, a mere reorganization of priorities. Christian conversion is a radical change of life, or, better still, a death that leads to a wholly new life, a turning to the person of Jesus and a total self-surrender to him as friend, lord, master, lover, teacher, king, and God. Such self-surrender gladly and permanently grants Jesus all the rights each of these titles implies.

This is why we cannot be disciples without first undergoing a major conversion, to be followed, hopefully, by countless others, every day of our lives, since no one can follow Jesus and learn from him the secret of divine life without first abandoning his old life and undertaking

the heroic road to sanctity—genuine sanctity, not the
Pharisee's counterfeit kind, but the sanctity of God himself, which expresses itself in his desire to redeem and
re-creates us in the image of his dear Son.

Where love is genuine, it has got to be shown, not
with words, but with the reality and daily acts of our
life. We do not even know who this woman is, although
some identify her with Mary Magdalen. I prefer to keep
her anonymous, because in this way I can more easily
identify with her. Nor do we know what she did with
her life after this episode. In this way she leaves open
a thousand possibilities for continuing to show her love
and gratitude to Jesus. Gratitude for what? For his being
what he is and for deigning to be this in her own town,
within reach of her hands and hair and tears. When love
is based on gratitude at knowing oneself loved and forgiven, the soul will never be at a loss as to how to express such love, through every word, thought, and deed,
but especially through a habitual silence that just wants
to admire and adore.

The essential thing is not to look away from Jesus, because, as long as he is there at the center of our souls reclining on the couch of our heart, we can be sure that we
shall not greatly go astray from his way. "Le regard est
ce qui sauve"—gazing is what saves, said Simone Weil
in an inspired insight, very close in outlook to Teresa
of Avila's definition of prayer: "I look at him, and he
looks at me." We must not remove ourselves from Jesus'
loving gaze or leave the radius of his watchfulness and
influence over us or hide from his love and forgiveness

out of a foolish pride and an obstinate sense of independence. The moment Simon Peter looked from Jesus to the waves, he began to sink (cf. Mt 14:30).

Simon the Pharisee did not think he needed Jesus' forgiveness, and Jesus therefore had no redemptive effect whatsoever on him, though he was reclining at Simon's very table. Simon had invited Jesus to his house out of mere curiosity and vanity; therefore, he could not learn how to love, and he never tasted the unspeakable joy of loving intimacy with Jesus. And how much those of us who are of the male sex have to learn about devotion from this ardent woman, sensual in her chaste ardor and longing to have an intimate contact of her whole human person with Jesus' sacred humanity and, through his flesh, to embrace and kiss Divinity itself. If men expect women to identify with an apostle or a blind man, with all the more reason male Christians ought to identify with this woman, who is perhaps the most ardent image in all of Scripture of the soul in search for God, the historical realization within Jesus' earthly lifetime of the Bride of the Canticle. As such, the woman is a living icon of the Church herself and of each individual Christian soul.

One last point: to the very end the grumblers have no rest, those like Simon who do not wish to admit God to intimacy. "Let God stay in his heaven, and we will take care of the earth!", they seem to imply. Such people are scandalized that Jesus should forgive sins, because they refuse to believe what the woman sees with the eyes of her soul: that Jesus is *Emmanuel*, God-with-us. They cannot bear to think that the one seated at table with them is God. Such divine nearness upsets and irritates them, because they are not prepared to submit to the process of conversion that has brought such joy to this woman. However, while they become vainly agitated, Jesus says to her: "Your faith has saved you; go in peace." The scene that had begun with tears of repentance ends with the smile and joy of a peace that only God can give.

"Only the loved person lives in peace", a wise monk has beautifully observed.[7] So Simon & Co. remain imprisoned, victims of their own prejudices and their refusal of love, incapable of feeling the deep emotions that only God can occasion in a human heart. And there they continue archetypically to this very day, stuck in their refusal, discussing and murmuring among themselves, grumbling with cynicism and disbelief, while the woman followed Jesus toward the glory of the Kingdom. I, for my part, have no doubt that she became one of those generous *discipulæ*, women disciples whom Luke mentions immediately after our passage: Mary Magdalen, Joanna the wife of Chuza (Herod's steward), Susanna, "and many others" who were with Jesus and followed him along with the Twelve, providing "for them out of their means" as Jesus "went on through cities and villages, preaching and bringing the good news of the kingdom of God".[8]

---

[7] Bernard Bonowitz, "Brazil, Monks, and Peace", in *A.I.M. Bulletin*, no. 69 (2000), 95.

[8] Lk 8:1–3.

6

THE ABANDONED PITCHER

T HE EPISODE of the Samaritan woman in John offers
us a synthesis of all the previous stages of discipleship we have been exploring: first, the free, spontaneous,
and mysterious call of Jesus; then, the learning of trust
through the experience of fear; thirdly, the baring before
Jesus of all our needs and sufferings; fourthly, the recip-
rocation of God's love for us by accepting his forgiveness
and pouring out our soul to him. But the present episode
adds a fifth and final dimension not seen before: that we
must ourselves become evangelists out of our experience
of conversion.

This text is quite long, and we cannot analyze all its
details. We will therefore select those aspects most suited
to our theme:

> Now when the Lord knew that the Pharisees had heard
> that Jesus was making and baptizing more disciples than
> John (although Jesus himself did not baptize, but only
> his disciples), he left Judea and departed again to Galilee.
> He had to pass through Samaria. So he came to a city of
> Samaria, called Sychar, near the field that Jacob gave to his
> son Joseph. Jacob's well was there, and so Jesus, wearied
> as he was with his journey, sat down beside the well. It
> was about the sixth hour.

There came a woman of Samaria to draw water. Jesus said to her, "Give me a drink." For his disciples had gone away into the city to buy food. The Samaritan woman said to him, "How is it that you, a Jew, ask a drink of me, a woman of Samaria?" For Jews [i.e., Judeans] have no dealings with Samaritans. Jesus answered her, "If you knew the gift of God, and who it is that is saying to you, 'Give me a drink,' you would have asked him and he would have given you living water." The woman said to him, "Sir, you have nothing to draw with, and the well is deep; where do you get that living water? Are you greater than our father Jacob, who gave us the well, and drank from it himself, and his sons, and his cattle?" Jesus said to her, "Every one who drinks of this water will thirst again, but whoever drinks of the water that I shall give him will never thirst; the water that I shall give him will become in him a spring of water welling up to eternal life." The woman said to him, "Sir, give me this water, that I may not thirst, nor come here to draw."

Jesus said to her, "Go, call your husband, and come here." The woman answered him, "I have no husband." Jesus said to her, "You are right in saying, 'I have no husband'; for you have had five husbands, and he whom you now have is not your husband; this you said truly." The woman said to him, "Sir, I perceive that you are a prophet. . . . I know that Messiah is coming (he who is called Christ); when he comes, he will show us all things." Jesus said to her, "I who speak to you am he."

Just then his disciples came. They marveled that he was talking with a woman, but none said, "What do you wish?" or, "Why are you talking with her?" So the woman left her water jar, and went away into the city, and said to the people, "Come, see a man who told me all that I ever did. Can this be the Christ?" They went out of the city and were coming to him. . . .

Many Samaritans from that city believed in him because of the woman's testimony, "He told me all that I ever did." So when the Samaritans came to him, they asked him to stay with them; and he stayed there two days. And many more believed because of his word. They said to the woman, "It is no longer because of your words that we believe, for we have heard for ourselves, and we know that this is indeed the Savior of the world."[1]

This is, by any standard, a great poetic and narrative text, which would occupy a rightful place in even the most selective and slender anthology of the best in world literature. In the first place, we may be surprised to see so mystical a writer as Saint John give us such a precise setting for the episode: he goes out of his way to set it in a very concrete geographical, social, religious, and psychological context, focusing like a masterful writer on the precise moment on a certain day when this woman's life intersects with the life of Jesus, in very particular circumstances.

Geographically, Jesus is going from Judea in the south to Galilee in the north, trying to avoid a conflict with the religious authorities by making himself scarce. He feels

[1] Jn 4:1–19, 25–30, 39–42.

harassed by the leaders' envy and fear resulting from his popularity with the crowds. Between Judea and Galilee lies Samaria. As the crow flies there are about thirty-three miles between Jerusalem and Sychar, the little Samaritan hamlet where Jesus arrives at noon. John wants us to feel the heat and Jesus' exhaustion, hunger, and thirst. Only the Roman occupying forces and the rich had horses, and Jesus and his disciples were poor, and so they walked. The incarnate Word, omnipotent God coming to us from the bosom of the Father, is exhausted with the work of redemption. The text says that Jesus is κεκοπιακὼς ἐκ τῆς ὁδοιπορίας, literally "exhausted with the labor of wayfaring", and it is enlightening to note that the same word used here for "exhausted with labor" was used by Jesus in Matthew when he invited all those who "labor" to come to him.[2] He can give lasting and substantial consolation not only because he is God but because he is a God incarnate who is himself fatigued by his effort to redeem.

In the *Dies iræ* we remember this divine exhaustion as we exclaim to him with gratitude: "Quærens me sedisti lassus"—As you sought for me you sat exhausted. "For me": each of us is truly the Samaritan woman at the well. Jesus is worn out by persevering among the children of Adam and Eve, since he is subject to their identical physical, psychic, and social circumstances and stresses. He is

[2] Cf. Mt 11:28: πάντες οἱ κοπιῶντες.

fleeing from his enemies, avoiding for the time being any open conflict, although precisely this will one day take him to the Cross. For now he still has too much necessary work to accomplish. From the outset the mention of "the well of Jacob" announces discreetly the essential theme of the narrative: that, underneath all ordinary appearances, deep below all difficulty and bitterness, all efforts and exhaustion imposed by love, there flows hiddenly and silently the life-giving *water* of God's merciful presence.

Who could recognize in this man—sweaty, tired, thirsty, and surely dirty from the road—the Redeemer of the world in whom God created the heavens, the earth, and everything they contain? And yet, this very man, this needy pilgrim, is, as the same John attests in other places, the Light of the world, the Bread of life, the Way, the Truth, the Life, and the Resurrection. Contemplating this mystery, Saint Bernard exclaimed: "It is only just, brethren, that we should celebrate the Lord's coming with all possible devotion, delighted at such great consolation, astounded at such great condescension, set afire by such great love."[3]

It is precisely these hidden aspects of his identity that he slowly begins to reveal to the woman. As far as she is concerned, she is just going to the well for ordinary water even as she does every day of her life, and there,

[3] Bernard of Clairvaux, *Sermo 4 in Adventu*, 1.

on this particular day out of all her days, she finds Jesus, who, like her, is thirsty. What unites the two of them, what makes their steps converge, is their similarity of need. The Word of God makes himself weak in order to encounter us in our weakness, first as the silent Word of Bethlehem; now as the weary Word of Sychar.

Why is this woman going to the well at precisely the hottest hour of the day? Probably because she is something of a public sinner: she has had so many husbands, and the man she presently lives with is not her husband . . . She is therefore excluded from the company of decent women, who come to the well in the cool of the morning or the evening. This is the most difficult hour, the most solitary, the hour of the "noonday devil"; and yet also the hour of greatest illumination. And Jesus, too, is rejected, by the religious authorities and the majority of the people. Although he is ostracized because of his radical goodness and she because of her dubious reputation, they are nevertheless two pariahs meeting in the solitude of rejection. Shared rejection frees them to be themselves with one another beyond all social conventions. "Freedom's just another word for nothing left to lose", bellowed the tragic rock star Janice Joplin. Solitude, rejection, and exhaustion: Jesus and the woman share the same yoke.

Can we really deceive ourselves into believing that the structure and values of society have so changed since the days of Jesus that today we can be his disciples without often finding ourselves marginalized? This is already the third time in these episodes of the Gospel that we encounter Jesus' predilection for those who must live at the margins of "normal" society: Bartimæus (who spent his life quite literally "by the side of the road"), the sinful woman who anoints his feet, and now the Samaritan woman. And, of course, the most marginal of all, the very archetype of marginalization, is Jesus himself, who has no place to lay his head and whom the authorities seek to put to death. Even in death Jesus will be marginalized, since he was crucified outside the walls of Jerusalem, as the Law prescribed for the sacrifice of the scapegoat who thus carried away the sins of all.

So we see God begging for a drink of water from a human being, and a sinful one at that. On the Cross, too, he will exclaim, "I thirst", and soon after, as the surprising result of that thirst, water and blood flow from his Heart. Indeed, he is a thirsty God, a tired God, a God looking for the companionship and dialogue of one of his creatures. How could it be that God is needy? Regardless of how we may define God's nature in the abstract as impassible, immovable, and so on, we cannot fail to see that, in Christ, the one who by nature has need of nothing outside himself has nonetheless voluntarily *made himself needy*, but only in order to communicate to us the life that is his. This action of making himself needy out of love may well be the greatest and most astounding work of his omnipotence.

What God, who is Love, needs is to give himself to us, thus obeying the deepest law of his nature as Love, and he can give himself to us only if he succeeds in kindling within us the light of faith that then provokes in us the yearning for union with him. The only thing Love wants is to be loved in turn, and, to accomplish this, Love does not hesitate to humiliate himself and make himself a beggar: "Give me a drink", says the immortal Lord to his sinful creature. As we sing in the hymn *Adeste fideles* at Christmas, "Sic nos amantem quis non redamaret?"— Who would not love in return one who thus loves us?

The woman is beside herself with surprise. Even before knowing who Jesus is, she cannot believe that a Judean man is so much as speaking with a Samaritan woman, let alone asking her for something, which shows that at that moment he is dependent on *her* generosity and goodwill. The situation shows a breaking-down of the man/woman barrier common in the Middle East even today and involving all kinds of social and religious prohibitions. Men and women sit separately in the synagogues, and many women wear a veil covering their hair and face, except in front of their husbands.

In addition, there is the deep enmity between Jews (i.e., Judeans) and Samaritans, since Jews considered Samaritans mixed ethnically and contaminated religiously, because in fact much pagan (i.e., idolatrous) blood had entered Samaritan veins during the many occupations of Samaria by powerful foreign nations. While many Samaritans did return from Babylon, many non-Hebrews were also brought in by the occupying forces, and the Samaritans who returned were tainted with idolatrous practices and beliefs. Samaritans did not share the same canon of the Bible with the Judeans, nor did they pray at the temple in Jerusalem. Jesus and this woman, therefore, are violating a double and triple taboo—sexual, racial, and religious. And yet Jesus, in his own need, sees in her only another needy human being, and, completely overlooking all barriers created by man, Jesus penetrates into the inmost heart of someone who is herself the first to be surprised by the encounter.

"If you knew the gift of God, and who it is that is saying to you, 'Give me a drink.'" We see clearly here that Jesus' human thirst is the means God uses to manifest himself to us, to communicate to us his divine desire to give himself to us, and this real, human thirst of Jesus is the condition, as it were, for God to be able to give us the divine water of his grace and life. In a magnificent phrase, Saint Gregory Nazianzen calls Jesus *the thirsty fountain*, that is: the Fountain of Life and Love whose very reason for being is to give itself away. The bold oxymoron Gregory uses tries to babble something of the incomprehensible nature of God's Being as love. To suffer from the thirst to give himself as the life of the world: this is the whole secret of Jesus' Heart and the reason why he exclaimed, "Father, I *desire* that they also, whom you have given me, may *be* with me where I am, to behold my glory which you have given me in your love before the foundation of the world."[4] Such a

---

[4] Jn 17:24 (emphasis added).

burning divine desire can become a reality only if Jesus dwells in us and we in him through his becoming our very food and drink.

In every chapel of the Missionaries of Charity, we can read over the altar the two words, "I thirst." It is from participating through the Eucharist in God's own thirst that these sisters find the strength to spend all their days quenching the thirst of their Beloved in the persons of the poorest of the poor. No example could be more eloquent in showing the deep union between the mystical life of prayer and the active life of Christian charity— love squandered on the person of Jesus both in the interior of our soul and consequently exteriorly as well on those in greatest need. This is the fundamental insight of Mother Teresa, who admirably managed to turn such a purely mystical vision into the most practical of programs.

The cross-purposes we detect between Jesus and the Samaritan plot the successive phases of the soul's dialogue with God. This conversation is very much a paradigm of all prayer. The exchange of thoughts and hearts that they undertake over this well rises little by little from the most palpable and immediate realities to the most sublime and spiritual truths. "Sir, you have nothing to draw with, and the well is deep." The woman proceeds on what she knows. She does not pretend to understand more than she does. But Jesus does not lose interest in her because of the literal manner in which she understands him, nor does the woman herself tire of him because of his mysterious way of talking. In fact, she is fascinated. They both stick perseveringly to this intense encounter, which, beyond all words, is effecting a union of hearts.

Jesus wants her, through the experience of this world's physical thirst, to begin discovering the soul's thirst for God. Slowly she begins to realize that he is speaking to her of *another* water, of *another* well, and that if he does not need a bucket with which to draw water it is because he himself is the vessel, formed by the Holy Spirit in the womb of the Virgin Mother, that contained the Pleroma, "the whole fulness of deity" in bodily form, as Saint Paul says.[5] The divine life his Heart contains is the water that God is giving the world to drink. Without precisely understanding what Jesus is saying to her, the Samaritan knows that she does very much want what Jesus is offering her: a water that will forever quench the thirst of whoever drinks it. In this promise she intuits the liberation from her slavery of having to come every day to the well at the hottest moment of the day.

What at first was a symbol of the crushing heat that cracks the very stones—the Palestinian noonday sun— suddenly becomes a symbol of liberation: because this is the moment when the full light of truth enters this darkened soul. And, as we have often seen, the first thing that the divine light does in us, before communicating to us

[5] Col 2:9.

its own life, is to expose our sins, that is, the Light of Life must condemn in us the death that inhabits us as a terrible tyrant we have become accustomed to serve.

The great moral problem of the Samaritan appears to be that, in her search for love, she has had too many husbands. And her present "husband" really is not one at all. The frantic search for love, which often compensates for the lack of quality by sheer force of quantity, in the end has created only a greater void in the soul. After so many men, the woman finds herself alone, face to face with the Son of Man.

An interesting exegetical notation to John 4:18 ("You have had five husbands, and he whom you now have is not your husband") refers us to 2 Kings 17:24: "And the king of Assyria brought people from Babylon, Cuthah, Avva, Hamath, and Sepharvaim, and placed them in the cities of Samaria instead of the people of Israel; and they took possession of Samaria, and dwelt in her cities." These five pagan nations, which supplied occupants for Samaria, have been apparently symbolized by John in the woman's five husbands, to indicate the Samaritans' religious and moral perversion in the eyes of the Judeans, who had kept their faith and their race pure of foreign admixtures. The woman, personifying Samaria, and Samaria, personifying all sinners, together represent the general human slide toward idolatry, self-indulgence, and the abandonment of God's Law. Note, too, the sexual connotation of the expression "they took possession of Samaria". The fundamental question here is our tendency to allow ourselves to be seduced by any lover other than God. The present, sixth "husband" on call, who is not really a husband, would then refer to the current Roman occupation that in the end utterly destroyed Jerusalem in A.D. 70.

We then have a grand total of six husbands who neither singly nor collectively have brought the woman any lasting happiness. After so much flirtation with love, the poor Samaritan still has to draw water alone at noontime, still has to continue looking after herself. What an unbearable burden, to invest so much in "love" and get so little in return! But Jesus is the seventh Man, who comes to remove this burden from her shoulders. Seven, as we know, is the number of perfection, the number signaling the end of the search, the fulfillment of all desire, the arrival home. What at first had been the mere breaking of a double taboo—Judean man talking to Samaritan woman —is revealed at this point as something much deeper: If Jesus dares to approach her and speak so intimately with her, without her covering her face with a veil (note how even the disciples are a little scandalized: "They marveled that he was talking with a woman"), it is because he is wooing her in order to seduce her heart and persuade her to welcome him as the Bridegroom of her soul.

We necessarily skip over all the other numerous aspects of the episode to conclude with one final theme: the conversion of the woman from needy sinner to disciple and evangelist. Jesus has peered into the depths of her soul and revealed to her her own innermost secrets, above all her deep sadness at never having found a true love. But this revelation, far from frightening, depressing, or scaring her away, rather fills the woman with joy, the joy that announces the beginning of a new life. When he proclaims her sins to her, Jesus works a kind of exorcism that frees her of them. "So the woman left her water jar, and went away into the city, and said to the people, 'Come, see a man who told me all that I ever did. Can this be the Christ?'" The fact that Jesus has cleansed her soul with his gaze incites her to recognize in him the Messiah sent by God, the anointed Lamb who takes away the sins of the world.

The abandonment of the water jar, like Bartimæus' throwing off his old rag, symbolizes the newness of life that derives everything from Jesus, a life that no longer needs to carry the same crushing and absurd burdens or repeat the same useless tasks. Notice that, throughout the episode, neither Jesus nor the woman ever drinks a single drop of water, even though everything was set in motion by thirst of the body. The two have been refreshed and satisfied by their dialogue of love—he by making himself known and inviting her to intimacy with him, she by opening up little by little to the divine seduction and surrendering at last with all the jubilation and immense relief of an enslaved soul that exits to freedom.

Such liberation makes her hasten to her townspeople, the very ones who have previously rejected her. Now she cares little about her marginal status: the rejected one now breaks the barrier that Jesus has first broken in approaching her, but now in order to proclaim to one and all what she has found. "Many Samaritans from that city believed in him because of the woman's testimony." But this new disciple, who has drunk in Jesus' essential teaching in what could be called a very accelerated crash course, is only an ambassador, the precursor who is followed by Jesus' personal presence. Her personal witness has opened up hearts and ears, preparing people to receive Jesus in person. She makes herself into a pure instrument of God's love; now she seems consumed with one desire: to love Jesus and bring others to him.

The true disciple rejoices at nothing more than at hearing what the woman heard in the end: "It is no longer because of your words that we believe, for we have heard for ourselves, and we know that this is indeed the Savior of the world." What greater joy could be ours, too, than to know that many others may come to share in our own delight at having been found by Jesus?

In her poem "At Jacob's Well", the contemporary poet Elizabeth A. Nelson offers us a most memorable poetic exegesis of the passage we have been pondering. I quote it here in full at the conclusion of this meditation, because reading it will surely leave in our soul what must be very close to the resonances intended by Jesus himself. So powerful can poetry become when it puts itself at the service of loving prayer. In particular, the poem provides a magnificent solution to the puzzle of the abandoned pitcher:

Here's what I want to know about the woman
carrying her water-jar to Jacob's well
outside the town of Sychar, in Samaria:
what charms, what freshness bubbled up
from which corner of her heart, and made her the oasis
that she was? Five husbands and then a lover
come one by one to slake their thirst in her,
and still some water-truce holds in Sychar, protects
this frank green spring from all polluting shame;
and now another thirsty man, this foreigner,
sits asking, and again her charms bubble up
like the water, like her questions. Could that be
what enchants them all, her way of asking
straight to the heart of things? And did she know,
before he spoke, how long her heart had thirsted
to be answered the same way? Hear the dance
of their talk, these strangers, as they sit together
on the path to Jacob's well, speak in circles
around the deep water: thirst and drinking,
husbands and lovers, mountain and temple,
Spirit and truth—askings and answers
bowing in, leaning back, swayed and spun
to the beat of two hidden drums. Here's what
I wonder about the woman, dancing back now
to the village, her water-jar left behind
for him to drink from: did she notice
what the disciples half-saw, how deep he had drunk
from their talk, from their dance? See the gleam
in his dark eyes, like sunlight sparking deep

on well-water; see his toes tap inside dusty sandals
in time to the dancer's steps; now see him rise
and laugh, shake his head, rinsed by her charms,
sated by her questions, enchanted by her thirsty
generous heart, a vessel after his own heart,
a dancer who matches his own steps in the dance
of ask and answer, of Spirit courting soul.[6]

[6] I thank my friend Elizabeth A. Nelson for her generous permission to quote her poem here.

7

BETWEEN THE ASCENSION AND PENTECOST

A LL ALONG we have been speaking about "disciples" and "apostles", always in the plural. No one can be a disciple or an apostle in isolation. Being a member of a group, of a body, is an essential condition for discipleship. How, then, does God make us to be *Church*, which is the proper name for this group and body? How does it feel to belong to the Church? What must the apostles and the disciples have felt during the time between the Ascension and Pentecost, which was the privileged period when the Holy Spirit, by shaping them into the Church, completed within them what Jesus had begun as teacher and friend?

The time between the Ascension and Pentecost is both full of joy and fraught with a peculiar sort of anxiety. Let us examine this question in our present passage, Luke 24:36–53:

Jesus himself stood among them, and said to them, "Peace to you." But they were startled and frightened, and supposed that they saw a spirit. And he said to them, "Why are you troubled, and why do questionings rise in your hearts? See my hands and my feet, that it is I myself; handle me, and see; for a spirit has not flesh and bones as you see that I have." And when he had said this he showed them his hands and his feet. And while they still disbelieved for joy, and wondered, he said to them, "Have you anything here to eat?" They gave him a piece of broiled fish, and he took it and ate before them.

Then he said to them, "These are my words which I spoke to you, while I was still with you, that everything written about me in the law of Moses and the prophets and the psalms must be fulfilled." Then he opened their minds to understand the scriptures, and said to them, "Thus it is written, that the Christ should suffer and on the third day rise from the dead, and that repentance and forgiveness of sins should be preached in his name to all nations, beginning from Jerusalem. You are witnesses of these things. And behold, I send the promise of my Father upon you; but stay in the city, until you are clothed with power from on high."

Then he led them out as far as Bethany, and lifting up his hands he blessed them. While he blessed them, he parted from them and was carried up into heaven. And they worshiped him, and returned to Jerusalem with great joy, and were continually in the temple blessing God.

Simply consider the contradictory verbs that appear in close proximity to one another in our present passage. These verbs manifest a very conflictive state of mind on the part of the disciples: they are simultaneously startled and frightened; they are troubled and entertain questionings in their hearts; and yet at the same time they disbelieve out of sheer joy. They wonder and worship, and they return to Jerusalem with great joy. For the disciples, their former way of relating to Jesus is a thing of the past. Yes, he is risen, and he ascends to the Father, and they believe it. But how will they relate to him now? The time of visible earthly companionship and teaching is over, for Jesus is no longer there to answer questions; and the time of full empowerment has not yet arrived. This is a period of blessed communal waiting in trust and obedience, a period that appears empty, a great holding of the breath, but also a period that in fact is the time of greatest divine activity within the disciples' souls, a period of radical internalization when nothing appears to be happening only because *they* are doing very little.

Jesus can surely be counted on to bring nothing but peace and strength, but even in the face of such bounty the disciples are "startled and frightened, and supposed that they saw a spirit". The glorious wounds that he bears are a proof of life out of death and also of the fact that this one before them is the same Jesus they had known before the Cross as their friend and master. "Handle me, and see", he prompts them: the act of faith to which Jesus is inviting them is not to the Resurrection as an abstract proposition and miraculous puzzle, but to the living and present person of the Savior, indeed glorious, indeed already on the other side of death forever, and yet at the same time much like themselves and very much with them.

Thus, if Jesus urges us to recognize the truth of our full humanity—united inseparably with his divinity and now already present within it—it is only for us finally to real-

ize the incredible glory of the mystery of our own transformation: "When we were dead through our trespasses,
[God] made us alive together with Christ . . . , and *raised
us up with him, and made us sit with him in the heavenly places*
in Christ Jesus."[1] How extraordinary that all the verbs
Paul uses here are in the past tense, strongly stressing the
fact that our transformation in Christ is something that,
in all reality, has *already* begun, has *already* taken hold of
our persons and situations. In other words, we recognize
the glorification of our humanity in Christ only at once
to realize the real presence *now* of his divinity within us.
Paul is here stressing how very literally Christ's personal
Resurrection and Ascension to God's glory is also *our*
personal destiny and present identity as members of his
Body, because we are found *in Christ Jesus*.

This strange and wonderful Pauline usage of the loca-
tive preposition *in* followed by the name of a person,
Jesus Christ, goes against every normal pre-Christian use
of the Greek language. One would never say that Plato
abided *in* his teacher, Socrates, or that any Roman, no
matter how pious, had his life *in* Jupiter. Only a poet
could metaphorically say, at most, that a lover bore his
beloved *in* his heart. Paul invents such realistic mystical
language to do some approximate justice to the mystery
revealed only in Christ: that those whom he loves and
has redeemed henceforth can have no reality apart from
him, living and breathing and working solely from their

---

[1] Eph 2:5–6, emphasis mine.

location—not only spiritual and moral, but even physical and psychological—*within* the person of Jesus. Thus, Paul also affirms that "we who first hoped in Christ have been destined and appointed to live for the praise of [God's] glory [*in laudem gloriæ*]",[2] a function that by nature belongs only to the Son but now becomes also ours as our very life, in and through Christ.

Jesus promises the sending of the Holy Spirit: "Stay in the city, until you are clothed with power from on high." This staying and waiting is to give them a full sense of human impotence, the permanent condition of human beings until God bestows something of his own Being on us. The image of being "clothed with power" is eloquent. It hearkens back to Genesis and the human sense of nakedness and shame because of sin, and it evokes God's clothing of Adam and Eve with leather garments out of compassion,[3] in order to conceal his creatures' shame for the time being. But this promised clothing now is different, since it implies an imparting of God's own power and life. Nor is this just any kind of concealing, but rather, paradoxically, a very radical revealing. After the Father has raised Jesus from the dead and created a new Adam in Christ, that re-creation through grace is extended step by step to all believers, so that whatever has happened to Christ is now going to happen to us.

[2] Eph 1:12.
[3] Cf. Gen 3:21.

The Ascension contains the great mystery of why Jesus must visibly leave his disciples, thus creating a physical void in their midst. What they most greatly love—their risen Master—can no longer be seen, heard, or touched. Before departing "to heaven" (the place from which power will come), he blesses them with the hands that show the wounds of the Cross. As blood had poured out of them forty days before,[4] now light and blessing pour from them as Jesus' final, visible deed on this earth. This event marks a major turning point in the story of Jesus' relationship with mankind, because this blessing is as if Jesus were saying to them: "I leave for heaven so that your own hands may now become my hands, your deeds my deeds, your heart my heart." How else can we explain their great joy in returning to Jerusalem?

The promise of the Holy Spirit and the blessing by Jesus' hands have communicated the certainty to them that, even in leaving them visibly, he is not abandoning them but rather making room interiorly for them to be what they have seen him to be—by now having the same Father as he and the same Spirit animating their lives. They must now themselves *become* what they have learned to admire and love.

In other words, Jesus now ceases to be but one person in one physical body among many in the world so that the Church corporately and in every individual member can become the presence of his Body on earth. Jesus disap-

[4] Cf. Jn 19:34.

pears as single individual in order to fill the whole world with his presence. From now on, those who want to see Jesus, the Messiah, will have to look to the Church and her members—for better or for worse. What an awesome privilege and responsibility! Note in this connection how the very last verse of Luke has to do with joy and with praising in the temple. The temple plays an important rôle in Luke throughout, because the great question in his Gospel is: How is it that God will become present in the world in and through the coming of his Son among us?

Thus, in Luke 1:9 we see Zechariah entering the sanctuary of the temple. There the angel promises the conception and birth of the Forerunner, who prepares the way for Emmanuel. Later in Luke 1 we have the Annunciation, where the Blessed Virgin Mary is overshadowed by the Holy Spirit, in fact becoming thereby the living temple of divinity. The exact phrase there is: "the power of the Most High will overshadow you", very similar to Jesus' words to the disciples at the Ascension: "until you are clothed with power from on high". Then, in Luke 2:22, we have Mary, the living temple, bringing Jesus to the temple of stones to present her Child and the Father's to Simeon the priest, to be offered back to God, but now from within the reality of his human nature. It is no wonder, then, that Luke, in his desire to proclaim to the world this unheard-of new presence of God in Jesus, unfurls before us the ascending steps of the modality of God's presence among us:

1. temple of stones in Jerusalem (summing up the Old Testament);

2. Mary as living temple, in whom the Son of God makes human nature itself the house in which he dwells; and

3. the Church as spiritual temple: the presence of Mary among the apostles at Pentecost in Acts shows her as the living connection between the earthly life of Jesus through the Incarnation and the mystery of the Church as Body of Jesus.

In the Church the Holy Spirit brings about in a mystical and universal way what first occurred in Mary in a personal and bodily, as well as spiritual, manner. The connection between the coming of the Holy Spirit at Pentecost and his first coming to Mary at the Annunciation is the key to the Gospel of Luke.

The apostles go on to become exactly what Jesus had been: note the description in Acts 2:42ff. of them teaching, healing, praying, breaking the bread of the Eucharist, preaching, and eventually going to their deaths to proclaim Jesus, in the same way he had gone to his death for proclaiming his Father.

Returning to the disciples' feelings as they await the Holy Spirit, we note their desire to know times and seasons when the most hoped-for things will occur. Jesus asks them: "Why are you troubled, and why do questionings rise in your hearts?" It is as if he were saying to them: "You are not to know the Father's secret decisions; rather, you are to wait for what he wants to do with you, you are to receive power when he gives it, and you are to witness to me." This is already a great deal, and they are to be content with these tasks. What we want naturally at first, however, is to share in God's knowledge, which was precisely the reason for the catastrophic Fall at the beginning.

The believer must watch for this constant tendency to backslide into a testing of God. The promise of the Holy Spirit and of Jesus' return, together with their experience of his Resurrection, ought to be enough for the apostles to get their bearings in their own personal history and the history of the world.

We may therefore sum up the apostles' mental and emotional condition between the Resurrection and Pentecost thus: They have seen and been told so much, but they cannot now digest it. Their whole lives have been too drastically changed in too short a span of time. They are full of hope, expectation, joy even, but also of confusion, fear, anxiety, full also of questions regarding the when and the how of things. And Jesus says: "Put all that aside and hold on only to my promise and my command to be my witnesses. Abide in your need to wait until the Father and I send into your hearts the Holy Spirit, who, being our Fire, will transform you from the inside out!"

During the earthshaking event of Pentecost itself, the wind drives them out of the "house" where they have gathered.[5] This house is Luke's final symbol, indicating that all human buildings and creations have to be burst open so that God can make his Spirit and action present in persons. Just as the burning bush had been ablaze without being consumed, and just as Mary conceived God the Word without the fire of divinity destroying her, now the apostles receive the tongues of fire that enable them to proclaim salvation in Christ in every language. This is what God's power in us does, when we allow it to enter us by making ourselves available to it through prayer, obedience, and charity, when we empty our lives of other projects and wait for his grace to invade us. We can then turn to the world and speak boldly with our lives of the "mighty acts of God".

If these Galilean fishermen became fearless evangelists, if a young and humble Jewish woman became the Mother of God and held him out to us, the Magi of all times, for us to adore and serve him as our Lord, so, too, can we offer ourselves up to be transformed by God's Spirit, despite all our own weakness, doubts, hesitations, and sinfulness. This vital transformation of our persons into other Christs, through the power of the Holy Spirit, depends crucially on our recognition of Jesus' divinity, a truth expressed emphatically by Luke in the apostles' last act toward the visible Jesus at the Ascension: "They worshiped him."

[5] Cf. Acts 2:2.

The great joy that leaps up then in their hearts, their capacity for receiving the Holy Spirit, and the whole of their subsequent ministry, all derive from this great act of *adoration* of the Savior. Only because he is God among us, and only because we recognize him as such, can we ourselves come to participate fully in the power of his love. The fulfillment of our destiny to become fully God's adopted children in glory depends radically on our adoration of the Son and our total self-surrender to him.

8

THE DISCIPLE
CONTEMPLATES
THE MOTHER

B ECAUSE a Christian disciple is above all a Christ-bearer, there exists a deep and indispensable relationship between Jesus' disciples and the Mother of Emmanuel. By an ineffable design of his grace, God has appointed us to be the visible manifestation of Jesus Christ in the world, the visibility of him who is the Son common to the living God and the humble Virgin of Nazareth. It was she who first made him visible among us, this Virgin whose childbearing, in Isaiah's promise, is inseparable from her Son's labor to "save his people from their sins".[1] We, too, should carefully take to heart the angel's words to Joseph: "Do not fear to take Mary your wife, for that which is conceived in her is of the Holy Spirit."[2]

Now, this communion with the Mother of Jesus, far from being an eccentric and misguided departure from the purity of the Gospel, is precisely that to which the Lord Jesus is calling us if we would follow him perfectly.

[1] Mt 1:21.
[2] Mt 1:20.

When in Luke 11:28 Jesus proclaims the great beat-
itude: Μακάριοι οἱ ἀκούοντες τὸν λόγον τοῦ Θεοῦ καὶ
φυλάσσοντες ("Blessed . . . are those who hear the word
of God and keep it"), surely he intends a great deal
more than simply the observance of specific command-
ments. For the "Word of God", used in the singular and
in such a solemn proclamation, must refer above all to
Jesus himself as eternal Son of the Father, especially in
the context of an anonymous woman declaring Mary's
womb to be blessed for having borne him as Savior. Likewise, the Greek word φυλάσσοντες in this same context
conveys much more than simply "observing" or "keeping": indeed, its full range of associations extends to "de-
fending", "cherishing", "fostering", "safeguarding", all
meanings directly relevant to the conception, bearing,
and rearing of a child.

"To keep the Word of God", as Jesus enjoins, cannot
at bottom mean anything other than allowing the Holy
Spirit to implant the Son of the Father in the womb of our
souls, and then for us to give birth to this Word into the
world in union with Mary, the historical Mother of Jesus
and the perennial Mother of the Church. The kerygmatic
birth of Jesus into the world from the womb of the apostles' faith cannot be a substantially different birth from
the historical one that took place in Bethlehem, for there
is only one Christ Jesus. The "keeping of the Word of
God" in this sense is in full harmony both with the Father's proclamation at the Transfiguration ("This is my

beloved Son . . . ; listen to him"[3]) and with Mary's advice to the guests at Cana ("Do whatever he tells you!"[4]).

Both the Father and the Mother point to the incarnate Word with love and pleasure. The Holy Spirit conceives him in us, and the Word, bent on redeeming us, points to himself as revelation of the Father. Mary is the purely human form of the divine will to save.

To be a Christian and a disciple, then, means becoming Christ-bearers in the world in the most radical and literal sense. However, such a visible presence and communication of the total Jesus through us cannot occur without our being in constant communion with both the Father and the Mother of Jesus, the two origins of his divine and human life. The Holy Spirit cannot accomplish the fullness of redemption in us, cannot effect the conception of the Son of the Most High within us—and *we cannot become another Mary*, the Christian vocation in a nutshell —unless we seek the company of her through whom and in whom he is permanently present, not only among the choirs of angels in union with his Father and their Spirit, but also visibly and humanly in his Church and within the landscape of this world, so wretched yet so graced.

"Every one who believes that Jesus is the Christ is a child of God, and every one who loves the parent loves the child."[5] This is the descending order of love in John:

[3] Mt 17:5.
[4] Jn 2:5.
[5] 1 Jn 5:1.

If you love the parent, you must also love the child, which here refers both to Jesus himself and to those begotten by faith in his messiahship. Must we not also hold this order of love with regard to Jesus' human Mother? If we love Jesus as Son of the only Father, can we avoid, without a grave breach of all decency, loving his only Mother? We love Jesus for the sake of the Father, and we love Mary for the sake of Jesus and the Father, and thus our love for her is not based on whim or mere sentiment, but on the firm foundation of God's own trinitarian Being and of the economy of redemption he has wrought.

"Going into the house [the Magi] saw the child with Mary his mother, and they fell down and worshiped him."[6] It is impossible to find Jesus in isolation from the two essential communities to which he belongs by his nature as incarnate Word. In his divinity we cannot embrace him apart from the community of the Holy Trinity; and in his humanity we cannot approach him apart from the family through which he enters our race and shares our human condition to the full. "What . . . God has joined together, let no man put asunder."[7]

As the Magi find him "with Mary his mother", they "fall down and worship him". Note well two things here: first, that they worship only Jesus, but, at the same time, that in bowing down in adoration before him they must necessarily incline with reverence in the direction

[6] Mt 2:11.
[7] Mt 19:6 = Gen 1:27.

of the Virgin Mother who is holding him out to them and to the world. Thus, worship of Jesus is inseparable from deep reverence for the Mother by whose obedient faith he has come into the world and made himself available for our own adoration. Mary's faith has thus made it possible for us to adore God incarnate!

We surrender our whole being in worship to him alone and, through him, to the Father. But, in so doing, we render an homage of deep gratitude and love to her who first believed and, through her faith, has made our finding of Jesus possible. Nor is this finding of Jesus with his Mother limited only to his babyhood, when he physically had to be held and presented to the world by his Mother's arms. His dependency on his Mother is a sign of the manner of humiliation and weakness whereby the Word has chosen to redeem us, and this kenotic existence persists all through his work of redemption and into our own spiritual lives today. Therefore, we must never forget that, since all the works of his divine love become efficacious through the means of his human body, emotions, will, intellect, and Heart, consequently the Mother who gave him the gift of her humanity is also continuously present in his every work even when she is invisible to us.

Especially at the moment when he sheds all his blood on the Cross, we must remember that this very blood has no other source than his Mother's body. His Father gave him the will to die for us, but Mary gave him the body and the blood to perfect and consummate the sacrifice. Mary alone gave Jesus the blood with which to drown man's sin!

We must meditate deeply on the mystery of natural human motherhood, femininity, and childhood in order to develop on that basis the full understanding of how God chose to redeem us. And a major part of that mystery is the manner in which a child—and this Child most especially, since he has no human father!—derives all its being from its mother. Is it not striking indeed that both in Genesis 3:15–16, when God promises a Redeemer who would "bruise" the head of the serpent, and in Revelation 12:9, when the "ancient serpent" is finally thrown down to earth, it is a woman and a mother who plays an essential rôle alongside the central activity of the male Child, both as his individual Mother and as Mother of the race of his followers?

How could these two towering moments in the history of revelation—immediately after the Fall and immediately after the final victory over Satan—be divorced from the Incarnation, Golgotha, and Pentecost, pivotal events all three where the Woman Mother is likewise indispensably present? How, after contemplating all of this, could anyone say that Mary is in no way different from any of the rest of the redeemed?

Such an assertion would appear to be a grave violation, not only of orthodox Catholic teaching, but of explicitly revealed scriptural truth. Denying Mary a divinely decreed uniqueness in the work of redemption surely must result in a very skewed and prejudiced theology. Often it would seem that persons holding such an opinion are primarily motivated by an implicit but unrelenting anti-Catholic polemic, ingrained in generations of Protestant believers since the sixteenth century; but with a paradoxical result: that the defeat of a paramount Catholic dogma should be more important than accepting the full truth of revelation.

The Child's dependency on his Mother, of course, does not contradict what is equally true: that a child grows to maturity and becomes in many ways independent of his parents. However, because we are here dealing with the conception of a Child as a result of divine initiative, and with the corresponding response of faith by a Woman, it would seem that the forces radiating from Mary's first act of faith must extend outward, not only to the actual birth and early nurturing of Jesus, but indeed to his whole subsequent existence, including the events of the Resurrection and of the Savior's present reign in glory.

A conception out of pure power and goodness on God's part, and pure faith and sinlessness on the Mother's part, must surely produce a great deal more than simply a nine-month pregnancy and physical birth! Indeed, it is the beginning of the Body of the Church, the dawn of the Kingdom of God on earth and in heaven. Mary's act of faith and love, as the indispensable condition for the redemption, urgently concerns and involves each of those who have ever or will ever believe and become followers of her Son.

"A voice came out of the cloud, 'This is my beloved Son; listen to him.' "[8] "His Mother said to the servant, 'Do whatever he tells you.' "[9] Both the heavenly Father and the earthly Mother do one thing only: point to their common Son, Jesus, and command us to obey his word. Thus, the so-called "mediation" of the Blessed Virgin Mary can be properly understood only in terms of her unceasing response to and active coöperation with that coming to her of the Holy Spirit that resulted in the Incarnation. Saint Paul's "until Christ be formed within you"[10] cannot occur without her mediation. For, if she was necessary for the historical Incarnation, the source of all redemption, how is she to be less necessary for Christ's coming to us by the interior grace of regeneration?

The mystical application to us of the reality of the redemption must correspond in every way to the historical coming of the Son of God and Mary, for it was precisely for *this*, TO BE BORN IN US, that he came. And does it not contradict the divine economy and will that he should become incarnate in us without the coöperation of the Mother, when her active response to God was a necessity for the historical Incarnation? Can we give our individual and ecclesial *fiat* to God's invitation while

[8] Mk 9:7.
[9] Jn 2:5.
[10] Gal 4:19.

totally divorcing ourselves from her on whom God himself paradoxically chose to depend in order to become one of us? Would such an option not be trying to undo the redemptive wisdom of God because we think we have found a wholly uncluttered, more direct, "purer", and "more divine" way, like the Gnostics of all ages?

Why, out of an alleged zeal for safeguarding the uniqueness and all-sufficiency of God's redeeming action, would one want to *confine God*, after his work of redemption on earth, to a splendid isolation and solitariness he did not have before or during the historical process of salvation? He ceaselessly engaged patriarchs, kings, prophets, and all manner of insignificant people like ourselves to collaborate with him in mankind's salvation. Above all "in the fullness of time", he involved a whole cast of characters in the drama of redemption—from John the Baptist, Zechariah, Elizabeth, Simeon, Anna, the Magi, the shepherd, and Joseph to the apostles and disciples and holy women of his entourage. Each of these had a special and irreplaceable part to play in helping to communicate God's grace to man.

God, it would appear from Sacred Scripture, chose to redeem us, not out of a radical divine solitariness, but by involving many persons as collaborators with his divine purpose. This is perhaps most clearly illustrated when John the Baptist objects out of humility and a recognition of who Jesus is to Jesus' own request that John baptize him: "John would have prevented him, saying, 'I need to be baptized by you, and do you come to me?'"

But to this perfectly logical theological objection Jesus responds paradoxically: "Let it be so now; for thus it is fitting for us to fulfil all righteousness."[11] Does not this emphatic *for us* not contain the whole divine and human synergy God envisioned for our redemption—that sinners should coöperate in their own process of being redeemed?

If all of this is true—if God, that is, chose to redeem us by appointing many collaborators in his mission—what shall we say of the Mother, the obedient Virgin full of grace made by God in his providence to be the sheer and perfect ground out of which would grow the flower of our redemption, the fruit that would nourish us unto life everlasting? Shall we say that she was an "instrument" or "means" momentarily needed to carry out an ulterior divine design but left behind after she had served her function?

To say this would be to misunderstand completely the nature of motherhood in general and of this motherhood in particular, since the parent-child relationship can never be reduced to mere passing "functionality", and it would be unworthy of God in the extreme merely to use and then discard a person. No: God knew what he was doing when he chose to save us by sending his Son among us as a man, by selecting and preparing a Woman who would bestow her humanity on his eternal Son just as he was the sole source of his divinity. If Mary had ceased playing an

[11] Mt 3:14-15.

active and essential rôle in our redemption the moment she had conceived and given birth, we would have to expect that Christ's humanity at some point again detached itself from his divinity, having been "united" to it only functionally, as a temporary arrangement.

But this Gnostic enormity undermines and subverts the sacred indissolubility of the Incarnation. The logical paradox of "Mary, Mother of God", solemnly proclaimed at the Council of Ephesus in A.D. 431, when the Council Fathers reaffirmed what the Church had believed from the beginning, is of one piece with the other two fundamental paradoxes without which there can be no Christian faith: Jesus Christ, two natures in one Divine Person; and the Blessed Trinity, three Persons yet one God. The mystery of the Holy Theotokos underlies the whole mystery of our redemption—from the Son's conception in her womb by the overshadowing of the Holy Spirit to our own conception in the womb of the Marian Church, "until Christ be fully formed in us".

If Mary is once "Mother of God", can she ever stop being that? Or can she continue being that without our feeling tremendous gratitude and love for her who thus is the Bearer of our beloved Redeemer?

A major aspect of the mystery of the Incarnation is that, starting from the central doctrine of Christ's true, full, and irreversible humanization, we may then infer a number of important truths that need not be explicitly spelled out in Scripture, since they are really contained within the fullness of the already revealed central Mystery of Christ. For instance, the normality of Jesus' hidden life and childhood: by their nearly total silence concerning this part of Jesus' earthly life, the Gospels are in fact telling us that Jesus lived a very ordinary human life for nearly thirty years, almost the whole of his earthly existence.

Something similar may be said about his relationships. Scripture nowhere calls Mary explicitly either "Lady" or "Queen", titles which the Catholic tradition has joyfully ascribed to her since very ancient times. But Scripture is full of allusions to queens who are mothers of kings, and Scripture also tells us that Mary is the Mother of Christ who is eternal King of the ages. Therefore, if Mary is the Mother of our Lord (*Dominus*), then she is truly "our Lady" (*Domina*), and if Christ is King, then she, too, must be Queen, for this is required by the very nature of these biblical titles, which are relational in nature. What are we to call the mother of a king if not the "queen mother", and what would be the point of calling Jesus a king at all if, although he very much has a mother, we oddly want to limit the implications of that title by applying it only in one direction, that is, by stressing the fact that a king has subjects who must obey and serve him, but not as well that he has a mother to whom he owes his human life and who stands by his side, always supporting him and loving him in all his works and decrees?

And Christ does not disdain so to share his lordship

and kingship, because he did not disdain to lay aside even his divine glory in order to share our nature. If he had, he would not have become man in the first place and entered this necessary nexus of relationships. Christ is not a sealed eternal capsule fallen to earth ready-made from heaven. Christ is the seed of the Word planted by the Father in the womb of Mary, that fertile earth that gave nourishment and growth to the seed of the Word, that we may eventually eat of the fruit of the Tree of the Cross.

> When the time had fully come, God sent forth his Son, *born of woman,* born under the law, to redeem those who were under the law, so that we might receive *adoption as sons.* And because you are sons, God has sent the Spirit of his Son into our hearts, crying, 'Abba! Father!' So through God you are no longer a slave but a son, and if a son then an heir. . . . So, brethren, we are not children of the slave [Hagar, but also Eve, the "mother of all the living"] but of *the free woman* [Sara, but above all Mary, the "woman" at the head of the text].[12]

Twice in Luke (1:38 and 48) Mary calls herself ἡ δούλη Κυρίου—the maidservant, the handmaid, the slave of the Lord. To be the Lord's slave is the essence of Mary's being a freeborn woman, in keeping with her Son's manner of reigning as King by serving. The Mother of the King who is a suffering servant reigns, like her Son, by serving

[12] Gal 4:4–7, 31; emphasis mine.

as the sorrowful Mother: "And Simeon . . . said to Mary his mother: 'Behold, this child is set for the fall and rising of many in Israel, and for a sign that is spoken against (*and a sword will pierce through your own soul also*)."[13] When and where, we may ask, will this momentous prophecy be fulfilled? Surely at the foot of the Cross, at the crucial hour when every disciple becomes Mary's son, by the will of her Son, and she becomes the Mother of all believers.[14]

We Christians are indeed "children of the promise" made to Mary: "You will conceive . . . and bear a son. . . . Of his kingdom there will be no end. . . . And blessed is she who believed that there would be a fulfilment of what was spoken to her from the Lord."[15] Mary's deepest identity as perfect believer, in the infancy narrative in Luke, should be seen in connection with the explicit mention at the beginning of Acts, after the Resurrection, at the other end of the work of redemption, of her presence among those who believed.[16] The Holy Spirit who descends upon the whole Body of the Church at Pentecost, with Mary present, had first descended upon her singly at the Annunciation. Thus, Mary is the living archetype, the living link, historically and mystically, between the mystery of the Incarnation and the mystery of Pentecost.

---

[13] Lk 2:34–35; emphasis mine.
[14] Cf. Jn 19:25–27.
[15] Lk 1:31, 33, 45.
[16] Cf. Acts 1:14.

In giving her *fiat* at the outset of the work of redemption, she is both accepting God's gift of redemption for herself and prefiguring—and hence making possible—the act of faith of the whole Church still to come.

Now, if being God's servant is the very essence of Mary's identity as first among believers and as Mother of the Church, is this servant, the Mother of the King and hence herself Queen by divine appointment, going to be left with nothing to do in the Kingdom of Heaven? Mary, an idle heavenly Queen? Or is she not rather going to spend her eternity of bliss interceding for her children, having learned such fidelity toward mankind from the eternal Father himself? Indeed, for as long as there is one soul to be redeemed on earth, Mary will spend herself saying to Jesus what she said to him at Cana, "They have no wine", and to us, "Do whatever he tells you."[17]

In the parable of the talents we hear the Lord speak thus to the good servant: "Well done, good and faithful servant; you have been faithful over a little, I will set you over much; enter into the joy of your master."[18] Since the parable is clearly a portrayal of the final judgment and the Kingdom of Heaven, we are surely to think that the "I will set you over much" must refer, at least in part, to the work of loving intercession that the saints in heaven will engage in as part of their life of eternal praise. For, how could they become separated by divine bliss from

[17] Jn 2:3, 5.
[18] Mt 25:21.

the continuing work of the divine mercy on earth? And, if this is true of all the blessed in heaven, is it not all the more true of the good and faithful Servant of the Magnificat, she who is also the Queen of Heaven because she is the Mother of the Savior and King?

Surely it was this keen awareness of Mary's exalted character in God's sight, and of her queenly mediation before her Son, the King of Heaven and earth, that made a humble Elizabeth exclaim with loud and wondering exultation: "Blessed are you among women, and blessed is the fruit of your womb! And why is this granted me, that the mother of my Lord should come to me?"[19] Should not our inmost heart, too, leap up for joy whenever we feel the approach of the Mother of our Lord, since we know that she never comes to us alone, without bringing into our lives Jesus, the blessed fruit of her womb, who is as inseparable from her as she is from him? There is nothing that Mary does without its being undertaken under the impulse of the original and ever-active grace that filled her from the beginning, the grace that drove her with haste into the hill country of Judah to help her cousin. In this passage Luke has marvelously portrayed for all time the fundamental rôle in humanity of Mary as Christ-Bearer and ready intercessor, who comes to our aid even without our bidding.

Just as we say that love, grace, and spiritual realities in general increase by being given away, so, too, may we

[19] Lk 1:42.

say something similar about Christ's sole, unique, and all-sufficient mediation before the Father: The more it is participated in, the more brightly and richly does it shine in its effects. For Christ's work of redemption, his suffering, and his Cross from the outset were meant to be shared. He exhorts us to take up our cross and follow him, to watch with him as he watches in torment, to go after him so that he will make us fishers of men. He affirms that whoever listens to us is really listening to him, that he sends us out as the Father had sent him out, that he loved us and so gave himself up for us so that we, too, ought to love one another as he has loved us . . . "I have been crucified with Christ; it is no longer I who live, but Christ who lives in me":[20] such is Saint Paul's unsurpassable summary of our participation in the work of redemption.

What is all of this, what indeed is the life of prayer, if not the practical form of our own redemption as a result of our participating in Christ's saving work? To begrudge the saints, and above all Blessed Mary, the intercessory and mediating rôle assigned to them by God himself in his election of them would be like looking at love, truth, and goodness as if they were material realities that must not be divided lest we end up with less and less of them.

But Love wants to be imitated and participated in. And our love wants to be united with our Beloved. And so —in and with and through the power of Jesus and at his

[20] Gal 2:20.

invitation—we are to do what we see Jesus himself doing: working, suffering, praying, interceding, dying, and rising for the life of the world. It is for this that Christ came: to involve us in his saving work. And the first one to believe and, thus, coöperate with him efficaciously in his work is the all-pure and all-loving Mary, Mother of Emmanuel, "God-with-us".

BLESSED ÆLRED'S EPILOGUE: JESUS THE EMMANUEL

"Behold, a young woman shall conceive and bear a son."[1] Whoever believes that a virgin has conceived can also easily believe that she has given birth to none other than the Son of God. Therefore, Isaiah says: "And [they] shall call his name Immanu-el", which means "God-with-us". Indeed, God is with us! Until now it had been "God-above-us", until now it had been "God-against-us", but today it is Emmanuel; today God is with us in our nature, is with us in his grace. With us in our weakness, with us in his kindness. With us in our misery, with us in his mercy. With us by charity, with us by fidelity, with us by tenderness, with us by compassion.

O Emmanuel! O God with us! What are you doing, then, children of Adam? God is with us. With *us*. You were not able, O children of Adam, to go up into heaven in order to be with God, and so God came down from heaven to be Emmanuel, God-with-us. He himself goes to the length of being Emmanuel, God-with-us, and we find excuses for not coming to God in order to be with him. "O sons of men, how long will your hearts be weighed down? Why do you love emptiness and seek

[1] Is 7:14.

after lies?'' Behold the Truth is here! "Why do you love emptiness and seek after lies?" Behold here the true and firm Word! "Why do you seek after lies?" Behold Emmanuel, behold God-with-us.

How could he be more with me? Small like me, weak like me, naked like me, poor like me. In all things he has conformed himself to me, taking to himself what is mine and giving me what is his. I lay dead. There was no voice in me, there were no senses in me, and the very light of my eyes was no longer with me. Today that great Man, that "prophet who is powerful in word and in deeds came down to me, put his face upon my face and his mouth upon my mouth and his hands upon my hands",[2] and thus he became Emmanuel, "God-with-us"![3]

[2] Cf. 2 Kings 4:34, where Elisha, raising to life the son of the Shunammite, is a figure of Christ imparting the divine life to man dead from sin.

[3] These three paragraphs are taken from Ælred of Rievaulx's *Sermo in Annuntiatione*. My translation.